ONE DAY BEADING MASTERY

The Complete Beginners Guide to Learning Beading in Under 1 Day!

Over 20 Step by Step Earring, Necklace & Bracelet Projects That Inspire You – Images Included

- SECOND EDITION -

By Ellen Warren

Note from Ellen Warren:

Welcome to the amazing world of Bead Making! As some of you know from my other books, this has been a passion of mine for more than 15 years. When you begin making beaded jewelry of your own, you're joining a very long tradition of artists, craftsman, and designers around the world who use beads of all kinds to make beautiful, wearable pieces of art. Making beaded jewelry allows you to express yourself both through the actual making or creation of the pieces, and through the wearing of it once it's complete. There are so many different ways you can construct beaded jewelry with no special skills or equipment!

I'm thrilled that you will allow me to show you how to create several of my earring, bracelet, and necklace designs, many of which are entirely suitable for beginners. I'm sure this will help you in your creative process while furthering your skills in this art form.

The pieces presented in this book were inspired by different things, places, people, and events. Sometimes it's the colors of a flower that I think work beautifully together, and other times it's the feeling of something that I'm trying to capture. The type of bead art and jewelry that I make fluctuates a lot depending on what else is going on in my life. After my first child was born, I began making bird's nest jewelry to express this part of my life. When we moved to a ranch, I began making funky art pendants in the shape of owls. An extended visit to my parent's home in Florida inspired me to begin using shells and sea glass in my art.

Even the simplest jewelry can be striking and beautiful simply by the way that color, texture, and pattern mix together on a single cord. So whether you intend to begin making your own beads to begin the ultimate journey in personal expression, or you simply want to start playing with color, wire, thread, and technique, you can learn to create striking and unique pieces of jewelry with the examples in this book as inspiration.

Beaded jewelry is an art form like any other; your inspiration and ideas for color combinations or for unique pieces of your own can come from anywhere. Any of these projects can be used as a stepping off point for a variety of different projects of your creation. All you have to do is start changing the colors, sizes, and materials and see where it takes you. Beads and wire, wire and beads; there are so many different ways that you can combine these two things to form countless pieces of art. Not all of the bead and wire pieces that I make are jewelry, but a lot of it is. I like the idea of not only expressing myself through my art, but then turning it into something functional; a piece that I can wear out and show to the world, or a piece that someone else can wear.

Beads come in all shapes, sizes, colors, and materials. You can make your own beads out of clay, wood, shells, pieces, stone, or plastic (some of my favorite beads are made out of little plastic flowers that I drilled holes through). You can also find beads sold anywhere, with many of them reflecting the area they are from, such as stone beads near the mountains and shells near the beach.

Making beaded jewelry is easy, fun, and maybe even addicting. Even the tiniest beads add up quickly to become big, full, colorful projects. Start making your own beaded jewelry today, and open up a world of color, creativity, and personal expression that you may not have even known existed. You will likely find that with each bead you thread, your passion for this craft will continue to grow.

Let's get started!

TABLE OF CONTENTS

Introduction

There are many different kinds of jewelry, but one of the richest and most complex types is made from beads. Beads and beaded jewelry can be found in nearly all cultures with many dating back hundreds of thousands of years. Beads can be made of clay, glass, stone, paper, wood, plastic, and metal. They can be found in hundreds of shades and colors, as well as countless shapes and sizes. They can be expensive or cost just pennies a piece, making them accessible for nearly anyone who wants to start creating their own jewelry.

Making beaded jewelry is one of the most satisfying – and oldest – art forms around. You can make beaded jewelry out of any material, and you can make it to wear for any occasion. From formal dinner dates to funky girl's night out evenings, jewelry is the perfect complement to any event and any outfit.

Making your own jewelry gives you a sense of satisfaction that goes beyond a mere compliment on what you're wearing; it also acknowledges your creative side as well. Picking and arranging the colors, choosing the materials, and pulling them all together take thought and creativity to do well, even if you're using a readymade pattern for the design itself.

There are a lot of different ways you can use beads to

create jewelry. From wire wrapping to coralling, beads can be transformed into rings, bracelets, earrings, and necklace of any style, shape, or personal type of expression. These techniques can be used with beads of nearly any size and shape, from selecting a single color and size of bead to weaving together a variety of different beads made from a mixture of stone, glass, and shell.

In this book you'll find the basics of beading from selecting your materials to mixing colors and arranging your layout. You'll also learn some simple tricks for making your own beads out of paper, wood, and clay, and some more intermediate beading techniques to start challenging yourself with.

Included in the book are also patterns and step-by-step instructions for numerous jewelry designs made for a variety of occasions and suitable for more advanced beaders. You'll find pieces you can wear to work, dinner out, or for a casual outing with kids or friends. Each piece will also have suggestions for materials that you can work with, so you can customize each piece to truly make it your own. Begin with the suggestions listed, then try mixing different colors and materials until you create something unique to you.

Make all of them at once, or wait until you have an occasion that needs a particular color or style of piece to complement it, and create something to match. Either way, you're sure to amass a collection of different, vibrant, and beautiful jewelry pieces that you can wear every day.

Beading can be as simple or as complex as you want it to be, making it the ideal medium for people of all levels of artistic expression. Whether you intend to make jewelry for yourself, as a gift, or to start your own craft business, learning to bead can open up a world of different possibilities for you.

Brief History of Beads and Jewelry Making

Most people start thinking of beads and beaded jewelry when they consider both the Ancient Egyptians, and Native cultures in North America and Australia. But beads date back much farther this, all the way to the Stone Age.

Evidence of beads formed from pieces of shell and ivory have been found in caves dating back to the very earliest settlements. And while most of these beads were originally used to decorate clothing – sewn onto the cloth itself – rather than as jewelry as we know it today, this use sets the stage for beads as a form of decoration or adornment for a person. In fact, one of the oldest archeological finds is of some beads made from Nassarius shells dating back more than 100,000 years.

The Egyptians were the first to begin actually forming beads that are more similar to those that are still in use today, and to begin using these beads to form things like necklaces, headdresses, and bracelets. The beads used during this era were tiny, what would be thought of today as seed beads. And although seed beads today are made of glass, the original beads were actually made of tiny pieces of quartz that were fused together and covered in a glaze to give them color and dimension.

Other early examples of beads and beaded jewelry began showing up around the 9th century BC in India and other parts of Asia. By the year 800 AD, beaded jewelry was found throughout Asia with many pieces found in Japanese temples dating back to this time period.

It was not unusual during this time for beads to be formed of nearly anything that could be found. Stones, precious gems, pieces of shell, wood, and ivory were all used to give color and dimension to the jewelry. Many stones such as Lapis Lazuli or Carnelian were worn as jewelry because there were thought to have healing powers for the wearer, rather than as adornment or decoration.

Glass beads first began to surface around 1480 in Venice when glass pulling was first used. The pulled glass could be cut or trimmed into beads of all sizes, blending color and pattern and allowing people to begin wearing beads as jewelry for every day purposes, rather than for healing, health, or ceremony.

The word "jewelry" itself comes from the old French word, "Joule" – which means jewel. This word was itself derived from the Latin "Jocale" – which means plaything. This evolution of the word suggests in part that jewelry was originally thought of as a light, playful decoration and not meant to be taken seriously by the wearer.

Today, jewelry is worn by people of nearly every age, race, culture, and socioeconomic background. It can be used as a way to express yourself, to show your allegiance to a specific group or culture, or simply to make yourself look and feel good.

And while many types of jewelry are still made using jewels, and others are formed entirely from precious metals, such as gold, there is still a large array of jewelry made solely out of beads. By continuing to make and wear beaded jewelry, you're not only exercising your personal expression and creativity, you're also taking part in a long standing tradition dating back thousands of years.

Types of Beading

There are a lot of different ways that beads have been used to create various forms of jewelry and decoration. Beads can be strung, woven, or sewed, and there are several different techniques to achieve a variety of different effects.

- The most common type of beadwork is known as threading. This is the act of stringing beads one at a time onto a single strand of thread, wire, or nylon. You can get a lot of different effects using this one simple technique either by varying the beads, varying the length of the thread, or by combining multiple threads together, twisting the strands, or layering them.

- Coralling is type of threading that uses beads to create multiple branches combing off of a single row of beads. Think of the way that a piece of coral may branch in different directions. So using coralling, you can creating a necklace with several small offshoots or a set of earrings that move in various ways.

- Stitching is one of the more elaborate and complicated methods of beading. There are several different stitches including ladder stitches, brick stitches, peyote stitches, and spiral stitches. Most stitching techniques rely on seed beads or other types of very small beads so you can weave them together to form things like flowers made entirely out of beads.

- Loom beading is a method of weaving threads or stitches through a set of beads to create a sheet of beads. Bags, tassels, and any kind of jewelry meant to drape on the wearer is using woven using this type of technique. Unlike other types of beading, which don't need special equipment beyond the beads, thread, and possibly a needle, loom beading does require both a set pattern and a beading loom to create the desired effects.

Most people when setting out to start making beaded jewelry begin with threading. This technique is so simple that it allows you to work on things like color, texture, and design without worrying about the intricacies of stitches or the type of thread you are using at the same time. You may want to start working with beads in a variety of different patterns at first until you become comfortable with the various effects you can create. After a while, you can begin branching into different stitches to create intricate pendants, broaches, and earrings.

Beaded Jewelry Trends

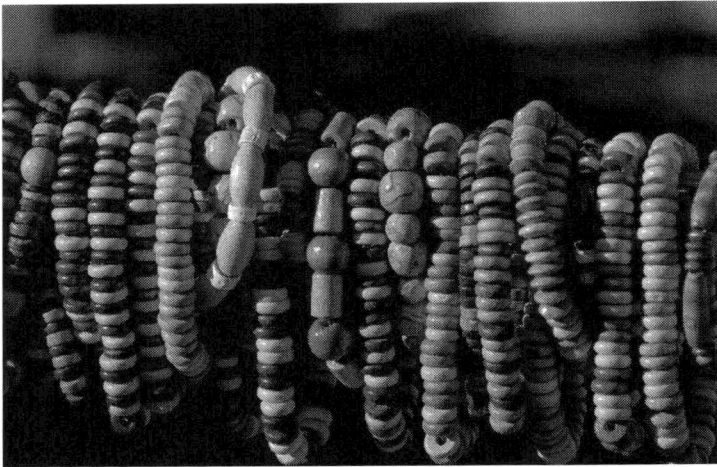

There are many classic, timeless type of jewelry and beadwork that never go out of style. There are also lots of different types of beading and jewelry that heats up for a minute, then vanishes into thin air. Remember the super long necklaces that everyone was wearing in the late aughts? You'll be hard pressed to find anyone still sporting one today.

With jewelry trends that wax and wane so frequently, it can get expensive to try to keep up. You'll need an ever-expanding jewelry case just to contain it all, too. This is part of what's fun about making your own jewelry. After all, by creating things yourself, you can:

- Bypass trends by creating unique, one of a kind pieces of wearable art
- Recycle old jewelry pieces by taking them apart and repurposing the beads in new and exciting ways
- Whip up the perfect necklace, bracelet, or pair of earrings to wear to a specific event, customizing the color and style to match
- Make multiple on-trend pieces in several different colors and materials for a fraction of the cost of what it would be to purchase just one at a store

Obviously, though, while everyone should have one or two trendy pieces in their accessory box to pull out on occasion, trends change so frequently that you can get exhausted just trying to keep up. That's why you should consider making beaded jewelry that speaks to you on another level – not just in color or style.

By choosing and creating pieces that can have a personal meaning, you can complement any outfit, while remaining true to your own sense of creativity as well.

That said, there are a few types of jewelry materials and methods that almost never go out of style, and that are always going to complement the occasion that you wear them to perfectly. We'll discuss a few of these along with the basics of creating your own jewelry and designs.

Layouts and Planning

No matter what you plan on making, or what technique you'll eventually use, every design begins with the layout. This is the method of arranging your beads in the same order or pattern that you'll eventually use to create the finished piece of jewelry. When you're working with a lot of beads at once, it's helpful to plan while the beads are still loose. Otherwise you can easily find yourself in a position of having a piece that isn't balanced, or that breaks pattern somewhere along the way. Your only recourse at this point in time is usually to start over, so a proper layout can save you a lot of time and frustration latter on.

Plastic trays are available that have narrow channels cut into them just for this purpose. It allows you to arrange your beads in the order you want them without worrying about them rolling away. You can adjust your tray size for the size of the piece that you're working on, and if you're creating a set pattern, you can start it in the tray to ensure that it will work for you before you start threading, without needing to lay out the entire thing.

Spacing

When you're taking the time to lay out your necklace, bracelet, or earrings, make sure you give some thought to the spacing of the beads at the same time. Spaces within a set of beads help the pattern come alive by giving the eye a chance to break apart of the larger sections. They aren't necessary; if you're creating a necklace made up of random beads or a bracelet made of all the same bead then spaces won't need to be part of the design. For other types of jewelry, however, spaces can add a lot of dimension and interest to the design.

Spaces can be achieved in your work in a few different ways:

- Using smaller, plain beads – sometimes known as spacers - between larger patterned ones to break them apart
- Using jump rings between beads to separate them and add dimension to the piece
- Using crimp beads along your wire or thread to stop a bead from sliding and leaving empty space on either side of a larger bead

Depending on the look you want to create, you should take the time to play around with the spacing. If you're using plain beads between patterned ones, consider using different sizes. You can also use varying sizes of the same bead to get similar effects.

Spacing is also a great way to get multiple looks out of one set of beads. For example, you could make a bracelet with patterned beads broken by plain beads of the same size.

Then you could create a second bracelet using the same patterned beads broken by plain beads of a much smaller size. You could even go on to make a bracelet using the same patterned beads but with spaces left by links or empty spaces.

By playing around with these different looks during your layout, you can find the one that works best for the look that you're trying to achieve.

Color and Pattern

You will also want to take color and pattern into consideration when you plan your layout. Jewelry doesn't have to coordinate or even contain multiple shades of the same color, but may designs rely on a mixture of just two or three colors to get the desired look.

Some tips to help you blend things perfectly include:

- Pick up an accent color from within a patterned bead and select some plain beads in this color to intersperse. This will help break up the design and keep the patterned beads from overwhelming the piece.

- Introduce some neutral colors like white, black, gray, or brown to your piece. For example, if the jewelry you are working on seems too dark or looks all of the same color, adding some white can lighten it up dramatically. Likewise, using brown or black in a lighter colored piece can add gravity and interest to the design.

- Consider the color wheel. There are several different ways you can coordinate colors by looking at the color wheel. Complementary colors sit across from one another – think red and green – and they create the most dramatic looks. Analogous colors sit beside each other on the color wheel, and they create more subtle looks, allowing you to blend multiple colors.

- Pay attention to the tone and saturation of the colors you are using. You can combine several different colors and shades as long as your saturation levels – how deep the colors are – remain the same.

When it's time to start arranging the colors, start with the simplest patterns; alternating colors or using a simple A-A-B pattern can give you a good place to start. If you're using a lot of different colors and textures of beads, don't be afraid to use a random pattern either, grabbing whichever bead comes to hand quickest. While you may end up with a run of three of the same color in a row, the overall effect can be striking.

Techniques

There are a lot of different beading techniques out there, many of which have been around for thousands of years. Often a technique itself doesn't really come and go out of trend, but sometimes a trend will necessitate using one technique over another to get the desired results.

Knotting is one technique that has been around for centuries and that is still used all the time today. This is the process of tying a small knot between each bead on a necklace, separating them very slightly. This is done for two reasons. One, if a bead is ever broken, all you lose is that bead; the other beads won't all come crashing off the strand to get lost. Typically, you see things like pearls knotted because you are more likely to want to prevent this from happening. The other reason is to knot between more fragile beads, to keep them from rubbing against one another and chipping or flaking.

If you're using any kind of bead, however, on a string rather than wire, you may want to consider knotting, particularly if the beads are large and heavy to help prevent damage to the piece.

Wire wrapping is a technique that comes and goes in style. Many different jewelry methods use wire to piece the beads together, but wire wrapping not only goes through the beads, but around them as well. There are a lot of different ways you can wire wrap, and some of those methods will go in and out of style. The nice thing about wire wrapping, however, is that it's fairly easy to unwrap and rewrap your piece to get a different look down the road.

Other techniques come and go very quickly depending on the style of the moment – chokers, long necklaces, dangling earrings, and chunky jewelry pieces all demand very specific techniques to do properly. If you find a technique that you truly love, try changing up the materials and style to help keep it relevant no matter when you use it.

Material Trends

Interestingly, a lot of materials that are used in accessories like jewelry take their cues from the kind of materials popular in home design. Think about it: for many years gold was the standard color of jewelry, until chrome and stainless steel became popular in homes. At this point silver and platinum became more popular choices for jewelry.

The same holds true for many other materials. Right now, there is a big emphasis on natural materials both in the home and for personal use. That means lots of natural stone, pearls, glass, and wood, as well as beads made from clay and cloth are all very popular in jewelry.

The nice thing about these materials is that a lot of them are timeless. Pearls, glass, and stone rarely go out of style for long, which is part of the reason why they are trending today; a lot of current trends are focused on sustainable design, and what can be used for many years to come without dating an item.

In addition to natural materials, warm colors like copper and bronze are very popular right now as well. Gold is also beginning to see a resurgence as a popular material for jewelry, although many people still prefer gold blends like white gold and rose gold over the classic yellow gold.

When you're choosing materials for your jewelry, consider how you intend to use the piece. Is this something that you're making for a specific occasion that you don't think will get a lot of daily wear? In that case, have fun using very on trend colors and materials as well as style. If you're making something that you intend to use as an accessory for many years, then choosing materials and colors that have been proven to stand the test of time may be in your best interests.

Materials You'll Need

Beads and beading materials come in so many different forms, you may want to experiment with several to discover what type you like best, regardless of trends or what may be currently in style. Remember, trends come and go, and the skills and techniques you're learning now are going to serve you well for decades, so it doesn't matter if a color or material that's hot right now isn't something you begin working with today.

It's also important to remember that beading and jewelry materials can really vary, not only in trend but in other ways as well. Not only do beads themselves vary tremendously in terms of color, pattern, size, shape, and material, but the materials you can use to thread them can also vary. Different types of beads also sit differently within a pattern, as well as move differently, while your different threading materials can also give you different end results even when using the same type and pattern of beads.

Therefore, it's important to consider your materials and how they will affect your end project before you begin.

Color and Bead Strings

While there are many specialty stores that sell beads individually, it's a lot easier – and cheaper – to purchase beads by the string. Many beads including glass, stone, ceramic, and metal will be sold strung together on a piece of nylon. Buying your beads this way is a nice way to see how the beads sit next to one another; round beads will sit very differently on a string than chips will, for example.

Some strings will also come with a variety of variegated colors mixed together. If you're unsure about putting colors together, this can be an easy route to take. Otherwise, consider laying out whole strings of beads beside one another in the store to start picking out the perfect colors for your design. Don't be afraid to select multiple beads of the same color as well, changing only things like texture or material to give your finished piece depth.

Irregular and Regular Beads

Beads come in multiple sizes and shapes as well as colors and materials. The biggest difference you'll notice, however, is in the beads' regularity. Stone bead chips, shell beads, and some glass beads will come in varying sizes and shapes within one group or strand. These irregular beads won't function the same way "regular" beads will, beads that have been machined to be uniform in size and shape.

Irregular beads can give you some very interesting looks, however, by giving you a randomness to the jewelry, even when using one bead or color. They can also be the perfect fit in some types of stitching or loom beading; an irregular bead may fit the corner or turn of a piece better than a round or oblong bead might.

Projects made with irregular beads tend to look a little more organic than those made with more uniform beads. So for those that prefer a more "natural" look, these beads might help you achieve the look you're after.

Wire

Many people prefer the use of thread, silk, or cord for beading, but you can get a lot of different looks by using wire. There are three basic types of wire: memory wire, which is difficult to shape, but retains that shape once you achieve it, standard wire which will bend more easily, but unbends easily as well, and woven wire, which acts like a cord, but with a metallic sheen. This type of wire works best for pieces where the thread is visible between the beads.

The key with working with wire is the gauge. Each gauge, or weight of the wire is assigned a number; the higher the number, the thinner and more pliable the wire. Look for 24 gauge wire for delicate wire wrapping or for creating multiple "strands" on a pair of earrings, or for 18 gauge wire to form a coil bracelet.

Jump Rings

Jump rings are fully formed circles of wire that are not easily unbent. You can join a bunch of them together to form a chain, hang several strands of beads off one ring, or use them as spacers between beads. You can usually find jump rings in two types: the first will require pliers to bend open and then shut again, while the second works more like a miniature key chain that you twist to attach to another.

Pliers

You will want at least two pairs of pliers when working with beaded jewelry. One pair should have a flat nose, while the other should be rounded. Ideally, they should also be two different sizes to give you some more flexibility in this area. You'll need the pliers to hold small beads as you thread them, open jump rings, bend the end of a wire into a loop, or to close a crimp bead.

Beading Needle and Thread

If you plan on using actual thread for your beads, rather than cord or wire, you should invest in a beading needle as well. Beading needles are thin, flexible pieces of metal with a large eye. To use them, you tie the end of your piece of thread to the needle, then use the needle to string multiple beads at a time onto your thread. Most of the time, you'll use a beading needle with thin cotton or silk thread. This is ideal for coralling, stitching, or any type of beading where you want to double back through a bead or around the outside of a bead.

Making Your Own Beads

In addition to the beads that you can find in craft stores, bead stores, and specialty shops, there are also numerous types of beads that are easy to make yourself. Making your own beads may not be on the top of your list when you first consider taking on some beaded jewelry projects, but learning a few different techniques is something that every beader should do at some point in time. After all, there are always going to be times when you just can't find or access the perfect bead for a specific project; having the ability to make your own beads can ensure that you never run out of materials to design with, as well as the fact that you'll always have that perfect bead right at your fingertips.

Making your own beads has a lot of other advantages for jewelry makers as well:

- It's low cost, perfect for those who are on a budget, or who make a lot of jewelry
- It allows you to create unique and one of a kind pieces that may be unlike anything else that could be found in a store
- It gives you greater control over the project as whole; if you are unable to find beads that match

your vision, you may be able to create those beads yourself to get the perfect finished look for your piece

Beads can be made out of nearly any material. Remember, that long before there were the types of mass-machined beads being sold today, that cultures and people where creating their own beads out a variety of different materials.

Wood Beads

Add a very lightweight, rustic, and often colorful touch to your jewelry with wooden beads. Making wooden beads is extremely simple, and can be done with objects you find in and around your home.

What you need:

- Several branches or sticks ranging in thickness from 1/8 inch to ½ inch
- Metal or wood trimmers
- Drill with a 1/16 inch bit
- Paint of your choosing

What to do:

1. Cut the branches or sticks into pieces ranging from ½ to 1 inch in length

2. Peel the bark from some of the pieces – you may want experiment with leaving the bark on some of your beads for additional texture
3. Drill vertically down the center of each piece of wood
4. Paint the exterior of the beads

Wooden beads are very light and easy to work with. You can mix them with other materials for a very unique and personal piece.

Shell Beads

If you live near the beach, you can make your own beads right out of the shells you find there. This technique works not only for small, whole shells but for those numerous tiny shell pieces that are often found all over the water's edge. Shell beads can add a lot of dimension, and mixed with things like glass and stone can make some beautiful vacation-style necklaces.

What you need:

- Shells or shell fragments of all sizes
- Diamond or carbide-tipped drill bit of about 1/16-inch in size
- Cooling oil
- Pliers

- Piece of wood block

What to do:

1. Grasp the piece of shell or shell fragment between the pliers.
2. Dip the end of the drill bit into the cooling oil.
3. Hold the piece of shell firmly against the wood block so the part you are drilling is in contact with the wood.
4. Set your drill to a high speed and drill quickly straight down through the shell until it reaches the wood belong.

Polymer Clay Beads

Working with polymer clay can give you endless colorful beads of all shapes and sizes. Polymer clay is a plastic-based clay that you bake in the oven. It starts out very stiff, but eventually softens in the warmth of your hands to become a pliable, elastic clay that you can cut and shape.

Polymer clay is great for making round beads of any color or size for a quick, inexpensive project. If you purchase molds as well, you can press the clay into the shape of flowers, animals, objects, and other shapes that you can turn into beads before baking by pressing a metal tool through the clay to make a hole.

There are numerous ways you can create beads using polymer clay, whether blending different colors together to get marbled looks, or using the "tubing" method of creating flat discs with patterns in the center. If you have an idea in mind and can't find beads in the right size, color, or shape, using polymer clay and a mold can often get you the exact bead you had in mind.

Paper Beads

If you want to create a colorful, fun, and unique necklace or bracelet for just one or a few wears, consider making some paper beads. Paper beads are very easy and fun to make, and take just a few minutes per bead to create. Like other types of beads you can make yourself, you can create paper beads in a wide variety of different colors, sizes, and patterns by varying the paper you use.

What you need:

- Patterned or plain paper
- Scissors
- Wooden dowel about 1/8-inch in diameter
- Glue
- Varnish

What to do:

1. Cut the paper into triangles. The wider the base of your triangle, the longer the bead will be. The

longer the triangle, the thicker your bead will be. Play around with different sized triangles until you find the right one for your needs.

2. But a dab of glue onto the outside wide edge of a triangle.

3. Put the inside wide edge of the triangle against the dowel and wrap the triangle around over and over, sticking the inside of the paper to the glue you applied to the outside as you make your first pass.

4. Continue wrapping until you reach the tip of the triangle. Glue down the tip onto the rest of the paper bead.

5. Slide your bead off the dowel and let it dry.

6. Paint some clear varnish onto the outside of the bead to help protect it and give it some shine.

When you're done with your beads, you can decorate the exterior further by using paint, glitter, pens, or other materials. Things like puffy paint can be used to change the texture of the finished bead as well.

Jewelry Projects for Beginners

You don't need to have any special skills, or even an array of fancy equipment to begin making your own beaded jewelry. Because the beads themselves, as well as the pattern they are put into, can become the basis for the interest and detail of the piece, you don't need to know any special techniques or to be an accomplished artist to create some beautiful and one of a kind jewelry pieces.

Threading is far and away the simplest way to begin creating your own beaded jewelry. All you need is the beads, the pattern you intend to string them on, and the base or thread material. This can be elastic for a bracelet, thread, or wire; ultimately what you end up using will be selected in part by how the piece will ultimately be worn.

To practice your layouts, patterns, and material selections, try one of these easy projects. Finishing techniques will be covered in the next chapter, and will give you options for how to attach clasps, or simply tie off the ends of a piece.

Simple Stretch Bracelet

There is nothing easier than making a simple stretch bracelet. There are no clasps or special equipment needed beyond the beads and some elastic. You can play around with different colors and sizes of beads until you feel comfortable with the color and layout combinations you're coming up with. Once you've made a few simple stretch bracelets, you can branch out by using the same colors and combinations on a more complicated jewelry design.

Stretch bracelets are a great beginner project, but that

doesn't mean that you can't make something beautiful and fun to wear. Introducing spacers, playing around with color and size of bead, and even making a bracelet that wraps around your wrist a few times can all be great introductions into making more complicated jewelry designs. Depending on the beads you use, you could create a bracelet that perfect for anything from a day at the office to a night out on the town.

What you'll need:

- Approximately 4 patterned beads
- Approximately 4 plain beads
- Approximately 16 small clear spacer beads
- Beading elastic
- Scissors
- Tape

What to do:

1. Measure out a piece of elastic that will fit comfortably around your wrist. Keep in mind that adding beads to it will make it smaller in fit, and you'll need it at least slightly larger than you would ordinarily make it to tie the ends together.

2. Tape one end of the elastic down on your table or work space to keep the beads from sliding off.

3. Add one patterned bead, followed by two small clear beads, one plain bead, and two more small clear beads.

4. Repeat this pattern until you finish with two small clear beads so that they will end up on the other side of the original patterned bead. Keep in mind that you may need more or fewer beads depending on the ultimate size of the bracelet, and the size of the beads you use.

5. Take hold of the end of the elastic in one hand and carefully untape the other end from the table. Keep the tape on the elastic, though, as it comes off the table to keep the beads from sliding off.

6. Remove the tape so you hold one end of the elastic in either hand.

7. Tie a square not in the two ends of the elastic, and trim the ends as close to the knot as you can get.

8. Slide the knot underneath one of the larger beads so it's hidden, and you're bracelet is complete.

Crazy Beaded Cuff

The crazy beaded cuff is a great project to use up a lot of leftover beads from other projects, as well as to get comfortable with the idea of random patterning. Because of the way that the bracelet turns and wraps multiple times, you'll need to adjust your pattern as you go to ensure that it stays even and balanced, while at the same time remains random and fun.

Crazy beaded cuffs are the perfect bracelet to wear when you're out shopping, having coffee with girlfriends, or on a girls' night out. Best of all, you can adapt the colors, textures, and types of beads to match any outfit or frame of mind. You can also adapt how large or small the bracelet is; bracelets that crawl up your arm will be more dramatic and eye-catching than those that simply wrap around your wrist a few times.

What you'll need:

- Memory wire
- Pliers
- Wire cutter
- Lots of beads in a variety of different colors and sizes

What to do:

1. Take one end of the memory wire and place it under your wrist.
2. Hold your wrist down firmly against a table to begin shaping the wire around your arm. Make several passes around your wrist, coiling the wire very

tightly around your arm. The wire will adjust slightly and open up when you are done; you need it tight in the beginning to convince the memory wire to hold its ultimate shape. Make a total of at least 6 passes around your arm all together, then clip off the end of the wire with the cutters.

3. Hold one end of the wire in your hand and use the pliers to bend the tip of the wire into a small loop. This loop will prevent the beads from sliding off the end of the bracelet. You want the loop to be large enough to do this, but not so large that it's highly visible behind the beads.

4. Begin threading beads onto the wire. Mix up the colors and beads by pouring them all into a tray and grabbing them at random. You'll need to pay attention as each curve goes around that you aren't making too many duplicates on top of one another to ensure the pattern stays balanced.

5. Continue threading beads onto the wire until you reach the end.

6. Bend the remainder of the wire into a small loop like the one you made on the other end of the wire.

Your bracelet should now resemble a beaded spring that makes a wild and crazy cuff.

Long Necklace

There's nothing quite like a necklace so long that you can wrap it around your neck a few times for fun and variety. The key to this necklace is keeping the bulk of it to small glass seed beads, and interspersing larger beads throughout it. The final length of the necklace is up to you, but the idea is to make it long enough to wrap at least twice around your neck, while still giving you some length down the front.

A long necklace is something that everyone should have in their jewelry collection, because it works so well nearly everywhere. The best part about making it yourself is the fact that you can have a necklace that matches every outfit, as well as every occasion. Try using some semi-precious beads mixed in with high quality seed beads for a necklace you can wear to a special event, or mix in textured beads of different materials with more varied seed beads for a funkier appearance.

Seed beads do take some time to work with, as their small size will cause you to slow down a lot, but that just adds to the relaxing nature of beading. I suggest pouring your beads into a bowl and just reaching in for them randomly as you work so you can let your mind drift while your fingers are busy.

What you'll need:

- Beading thread and needle
- Round glass seed beads, medium to large sized
- Glass beads in a similar color that are at least twice as large
- Shells, blister pearls, or other interesting bead to intersperse with the others

What to do:

1. Measure out your thread to the length you want the finished necklace to be.

2. Tie your beading needle to one end of the thread, and knot the other end securely to keep the beads from falling off.

3. Begin threading several seed beads onto the thread followed by a larger bead, an accent bead, and another larger bead. You may want to play around with how many seed beads you use in a run. Count on at least 20, but depending on their size, you may want to use more.

4. Repeat this pattern of seed beads, large bead, accent bead, and large bead until you near the end of the thread.

5. Slide the beads up the thread away from the knot at the other end slightly and cut off the needle.

6. Securely tie the two ends together and clip off the excess thread so you can hide the knot between two beads.

Finishing Techniques for Beginners

Most beginners quickly pick up on the basics of creating different patterns and combinations of beads. What often stops them from moving on to more intermediate and advanced projects is the different techniques involved in finishing the designs.

Elastic and thread are fairly easy to work with when you are able to tie to the two ends together. But if you are making something with multiple strands or that is short enough to need a clasp, you need some way to join everything together and finish the piece.

Luckily, most finishing techniques are actually fairly easy to do, once you learn the basics and get the basic equipment required – a pair of pliers and some crimp beads.

Joining Multiple Strands and Adding Clasps

If you're making a multiple strand bracelet or necklace that needs to all join the same clasp, you have a few options on how you can do this. You can thread all the various pieces of thread or metal through the loop in the clasp to double back on themselves before joining them, or you can leave one strand longer than the others to thread through the loop on the clasp and double back to join the others.

Both techniques require the use of a crimp bead.

A crimp bead is a small, hollow metal tube. They come in multiple sizes, and you can often find them in a variety pack of different sizes of finishes. To use them:

1. Slide a crimp bead over the strand or strands that will be joined together.

2. Make sure there is enough room in the bead to accommodate the rest of the strands after they pass through the clasp and return, making a loop at the end. Alternatively, you can also use a crimp bead on either side of a bead to make a floating-style necklace with space along the wire.

3. Slide the crimp bead far enough down the strands to give you room to make your loop through the end of the clasp and pass back down.

4. Push the ends of the strand or strand into the crimp bead. It should be a tight fit at this point.

5. Grasp the crimp bead between the flat ends of your pliers.

6. Squeeze the pliers together tightly; this will compress the crimp bead and hold your strands together tightly. At the end of the loop you just made, you'll have half of a clasp ready to join the other half to close your necklace. Repeat with the other half of the clasp on the other side.

You can also use crimp beads on thread to secure the ends of a single strand necklace to a clasp as well. In this case, just trim the excess thread after it comes out of the crimp bead to neaten up the ends.

Wire Wrapping

If you're using wire to thread your beads, and want to add a clasp, there is often no need to add a crimp bead. Instead, you can usually pass the end of the wire through the loop on the jump ring or clasp a few times, wrapping it securely. This technique works best with very thin wire – 22 gauge or higher, but can still be done with thicker wire if the jump ring or clasp you are using is large enough to accommodate at last two passes of the wire to make a secure hold.

When you're done, just bend under the end of the wire slightly to double it back on itself. This will prevent the end from sticking out and potentially catching on clothing or skin while the piece is being worn.

Necklace Designs

A good necklace can really make an outfit come alive. Necklaces draw attention to your neck, chest, and face, and which can mean less emphasis on "trouble spots". Necklaces can dress up a plain outfit, add a much needed spark of color to the palette, or turn a work outfit into an evening one.

The following necklace designs run the gamut from those that you'll want to wear to work to those that are suitable for a weekend at the beach. Each one can be modified with a variety of different materials, or by changing the length of the piece of the placement of the beads. With each necklace is a suggestion for materials and colors, but feel free to customize as you see fit to create something that is all your own.

Chunky Necklace with Pendant

Every woman should have at least one fun, chunky necklace and pendant set. These heavy pieces are very eye catching, and you can make them out of any number of different materials. This particular necklace uses all one color to help tone it down a little. Where its fun and charm come from is in the heaviness of the pieces, the material, and the size of the piece.

I suggest using a really unusual material for this necklace. I like Honey Onyx because it appears to glow as if it's lit from within. And as a natural material, onyx is never exactly the same in each piece with lots of subtle variation. This helps ensure that while the necklace is made of one stone, it's anything but boring.

Any really eye catching stone or glass could be used, provided that you look for pieces that have something unusual about them. This could be the shape of the beads, or the luster of the finish. Stones like carnelian, turquoise, lapis, and amethyst all make good choices, but if you find an unusual pendant made of glass, feel free to mix this with any kind of glass, stone, or ceramic beads that match it in color to help set it off.

Because this necklace is so big and chunky, you'll need to use a fairly heavy gauge wire to hold it together. Nylon, string, and thinner wires won't have the strength to hold the pieces long term, which could result in the necklace breaking suddenly while you're wearing it.

What you'll need:

- One large pendant
- Enough large and small beads to make a necklace that will hang down to approximately your sternum
- 18 gauge wire

- Pliers
- Wire cutters

What you'll do:

1. Arrange the beads into the approximate pattern that you want them to lay in. This will be determined largely by the size and number of beads that you have. Position the pendant at the base, then lay out the beads from there. Alternating large and small beads is one method, or if you only have a few large beads, try placing them at randomly spaced intervals around the necklace.

2. Cut a piece of wire to approximately 2-inches in length. Depending on the size of your beads, you may need wire that is longer or shorter to complete each link.

3. Take the tip of your pliers and bend the end of a piece of wire into a small loop.

4. Thread a bead onto the wire so that it stops at the loop.

5. Bend the other end of the wire into a loop so that the bead sits tightly between the two loops and

doesn't slide on the wire in the center. Cut the wire shorter if necessary.

6. Take a second piece of wire and pass one end through one of the loops on your first bead.

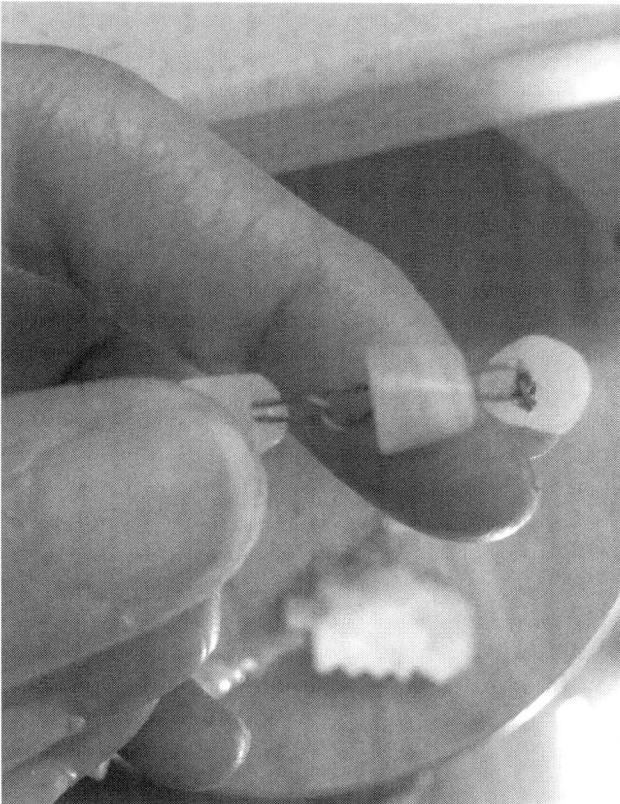

7. Close this end of the second piece of wire into a loop so that it is joined to the first loop.

8. Thread a second bead onto the wire and close its end into another loop.

9. Continue wiring the beads together in this method until you reach the pendant at the bottom. Attach the pendant the same way, but if you have a very heavy pendant, double up your wires here so you have two pieces making the connection.

10. Continue to wire until you reach the last bead.

11. Cut the wire for this bead about 1-inch longer than you would ordinarily.

12. Attach one end to the last loop in the chain and pass the open end through the bead.

13. Make a long loop with the other end so that the open end tucks back inside the bead.

14. Squeeze the loop sides together tightly with your pliers so that the wire doubles back on itself.

15. About halfway down this double wire, bend it at a 90 degree angle facing up. This will form a sort of hook coming out of the last bead.

16. Push this hook through the loop on the first bead to join the two ends of the necklace. While this necklace should be large enough to go over your head if it ends at your sternum, this closure gives

you the option of putting it on or removing it directly around your neck if you're wearing a hat or an elaborate hair style.

Casual Summer Shell Necklace

Sometimes a lightweight, casual beach dress needs something to dress it up a little after the sun goes down. That's what this necklace is designed to do; add a little fun to your summer wardrobe. This shell based necklace can be paired with jeans and a tank top or worn with a maxi dress. You can make it as many strands as you like; the more strands you add to it, the more wild and heavy the piece becomes. The fewer the strands the more sedate, although you want to use at least three or four strands to get the overall effect and not lose any of the flair that the design brings.

If you live near a beach, you can gather up an assortment of small shells and shell pieces to use in the piece, as well as any pieces of beach glass you may find. Just drill a small hole through each one to make it usable on the necklace. Otherwise, you can generally find long strings of matched shells and beads made of "sea glass" that you can combine with tiny charms and other things to create a unique and funky necklace that will make you long for summer just by seeing it in your jewelry box.

What you'll need:

- About 30 small shells and shell pieces

- Assorted glass and stone beads in gold, sea green, light blue, white, and tan – try to get an assortment of colors and sizes to mix in with the shells

- Small trinkets or charms to scatter through the necklace, these could be metal charms in the shape of shells or lobsters, or stone beads carved in the shape of birds − whatever makes you think of summer and that can add a little bit of whimsy to the finished design
- Jewelry thread and needle
- Two crimp beads
- Pliers
- Toggle clasp set

What you'll do:

1. Begin by figuring out exactly how big you want the necklace to be. Ideally, it should dip a few inches below your collarbone, but the more strands you add, the thicker it will get, so you may want to add a few extra inches to the length if you plan on using more than five strands.

2. Cut as many strands as you intend to use of your jewelry thread, making each one about an inch longer than you actually need it to be. This will be your cuts and waste; always give yourself a little extra to work with, you can trim later.

3. Make a knot at the end of one thread so the beads won't slide off the end, and tie the other end to the threading needle. A needle isn't absolutely necessary for this piece, but with the number of beads you'll be stringing, it will help keep your thread from unraveling at the end as you work.

4. Start stringing a mixture of shells and beads onto the thread. The idea is that you want this to be completely random. A good idea is to pour your shells, beads, and charms into a large bowl and mix it well. Then just reach into the bowl at random as you work to lift out pieces. Don't worry if you get two or three of the same bead in a row; this won't be noticed in the final necklace.

5. Continue stringing beads on this thread in a random pattern until you reach the end. Cut off your needle and knot the end of the thread, leaving yourself about an inch of open thread at the end of the bead run.

6. Set this strand aside.

7. Repeat with each of the other strands that you'll be using in the necklace. Have fun mixing colors and materials along each strand. If you want to, you can

make one or two strands slightly different – all shells or no shells at all – to help the piece stand out.

8. Gather up all of your finished strands together in one hand.

9. Hold them all by the knots at one end so that they point toward the ground.

10. Slide all the beads down to one end of their threads so that you're holding them by the loose thread at the end.

11. Cut off the knots at the ends and slide a crimp bead over all the threads down a little less than a centimeter.

12. Pass the open ends of the threads through one of the loops on one end of the clasp, then push them all back down into the crimp bead so that the crimp bead is up tight against the other beads.

13. Squeeze the crimp bead with the pliers to collapse it and join the strands to one end of the clasps.

14. Hold the necklace by the other end with no clasp so that the beads point down and slide down their strands tightly against the crimp bead, leaving you with some open string at the other end.

15. Twist the strands around one another loosely. The idea is just to tangle them up a little, not to make a tight rope.

16. Cut the knots off the ends of open string and slide a crimp bead on. This time, push the crimp bead all the way down the thread until it reaches the beads.

17. Slip the open ends of the threads through the loop on the other side of the clasp and push them back into the crimp bead. If necessary, pull the loose thread all the way through the bead and cut off the excess before crimping the bead.

18. Try on your new necklace

Bird's Nest Pendant Necklace

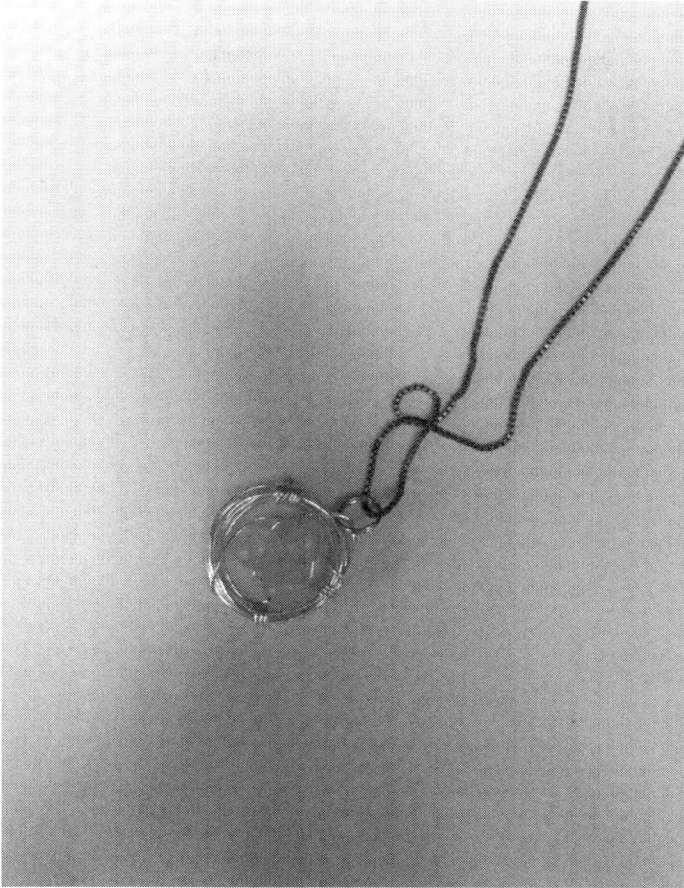

Everywhere you look nowadays, from television commercials to magazine ads, you'll see jewelry marketed toward mothers. Mothers and motherhood are more celebrated today than ever before, so it makes sense that from that comes a wealth of jewelry to symbolize the love between a mother and a child.

I came up with this particular design shortly after my son was born. I had dreamed of birds through the whole pregnancy, so I liked the idea of a small nest that I could wear. It took a lot of experimenting to find a design that balanced lightness with a "hugged in" feeling to it. The best part of this design is that you can change and vary the size, number, and color of the eggs inside of it. So if you have two boys and a girl, use two blue beads and a pink. I've made pendants with up to five eggs inside before, enlarging the nest slightly, and I've also made necklaces with as few as two eggs. Most of the time, though, I work with three eggs. Three fills up the nest completely, and there's something pleasing to the eye of the asymmetry that three eggs can bring.

I've also made these in all colors; yellow, green, pink, blue, gray; you can customize your pendant to your favorite colors so you can wear it anytime that you like. I've found that both pearls and beads made from semi-precious stones like quartz, amethyst, and aquamarine work best in this piece, but I've also used ceramic and glass when I wanted to get the color just right. Just be sure that no matter what type of beads you use for the eggs, that you make them all the same size to fit neatly into the nest.

What you'll need:

- 18 gauge silver-plated wire
- Pliers

- Three small beads, measuring about 1/8-inch in diameter
- Jump ring

What you'll do:

1. Lay out your three beads in a triangle formation, touching one another. You'll need to ensure that your nest is large enough to go around them, but small enough that they'll fit snuggly, touching the wire on all sides.

2. Take the roll of silver-plated wire and begin wrapping it around your index finger. This is just to give the nest its basic form; you can enlarge the wire by wrapping it very loosely to start or make it smaller by pulling the wire very tightly.

3. Wrap the wire roughly 20 times around your finger, then clip the end of the wire and slide it off.

4. Check the size of the nest by putting it over the three beads. Make adjustments to the size of the wire by either pulling the two loose ends to tighten up the coils and re-wrapping the loose ends, or by inserting your pliers into the center of the nest and opening them until the nest enlarges slightly.

Recheck the size on the beads and make more adjustments if necessary.

5. Cut a small piece of wire, about ½-inch in length.

6. Wrap this around the nest tightly to secure the nest in its current size.

7. Cut another piece of wire, about 4-inches in length.

8. Slide your three beads onto it, so that they sit in the middle of the wire.

9. Bend the wire up so that the three beads form a triangle again.

10. Cross the two wires one over the other and pull them down the sides of the triangle.

11. Fit the triangle of beads into the wire nest.

12. Wrap the ends of the two loose wires coming off either side of the beads around the nest to secure the beads in place.

13. Leave one of the loops you are twisting around the nest slightly taller than the others, so it forms a small space.

14. Open up your jump ring with a pair of pliers and insert it through the small loop you left on the top of the nest.

15. Slide a chain through the jump ring to wear your new pendant.

Fimo Bead Necklace

While it's possible to find beads of all colors and sizes these days, sometimes it's hard to find the exact color that you want in the exact sizes that you want. This can be further complicated when you find the color you're after, but it only comes in one size, when the design you're working on calls for two. In this case, one of the ways you can work around this is to use some polymer class like Fimo to make your own beads.

Using Fimo to make beads has a lot of advantages. You can blend colors of clay together to form a new shade that is just what you're after, and you can make beads of all different sizes as well. You can even swirl two colors together to get a marble effect, or layer a few colors together in stripes. You can even make beads using a mold to get different looks entirely.

This necklace will have you experiment with making two sizes of beads in two different colors using Fimo clay and stringing them together to make a chunky, fun necklace for a night out. You can use any two colors of clay that you want, or mix together some colors to come up with your own shade or a swirled, marble look.

The reason I'm suggesting Fimo instead of Sculpey or another polymer clay is because Fimo tends to be a little bit softer and easier to work with. Some of the colors of Sculpey tend to be flaky and brittle until you work them for a while, so if this is your first time using a polymer clay, you'll find Fimo to be the easier route.

What you'll need:

- At least two colors of Fimo clay
- Bamboo skewer like you would use for Shish Kabob
- Aluminum foil
- Baking tray
- Beading thread and needle
- Ribbon of your choice of color

What you'll do:

1. Begin by softening your clay. Fimo gets softer when worked in warm hands, so press, knead, roll, and otherwise work the clay between your fingers until it is very soft and pliable.

2. Divide each color of clay into 10 equal sections. Further divide five sections of each color in half.

3. Take each of the sections one at a time and roll it into a ball. You can use your hands or roll the clay on a flat surface until it takes the shape you're after. Set each ball aside until you've rolled them all up.

4. Pick up a ball gently between two fingers of your non-dominant hand.

5. Take the bamboo skewer with your other hand and push it straight through the clay ball to the other

side. Pull it out again and smooth down the raw edges of the bead around the hole.

6. Place the finished bead onto a baking sheet lined with aluminum foil.

7. Repeat for the other beads.

8. Bake the beads according to the instructions on the Fimo packaging and let them cool.

9. Begin threading your beads onto the beading thread, holding the thread upside down so that the beads fall against the knot at the end.

10. Thread your beads in any pattern – big/small or alternating colors until you reach about 5-inches in length.

11. Now thread a small offshoot by using the smaller beads, and taking your thread around the last bead and back through the offshoot to the top again. Place a few larger beads and repeat. In the end you want three or four offshoots at the bottom of your necklace.

12. Continue beading until you balance out the necklace on the other side.

13. Tie the thread on either end of the beads onto a piece of ribbon. To wear the necklace, tie the ribbon in a bow behind your neck.

Multi Twisted Strand Necklace

Sometimes you need a simple, yet interesting necklace to complete your office casual wardrobe. Pendants and big chunky jewelry don't always work in the office, and it can get boring wearing simple chains, pearls, and other classic pieces all the time. This necklace works to bridge the gap between fun and colorful and work wardrobe ready. You can use as many or as few colors in it as you like, and make as many strands as you would like as well.

The end result is a glittering, tasteful necklace that is filled with interest and color, but that is nice enough to wear to the office every day. If your workplace is a little more relaxed, feel free to have some fun with this design, working in several different sizes of beads, as well as several different color and strands. For more sedate work places, just stick to a single color and limit the number of strands that you use.

What you'll need:

- Large container of seed beads, either a single color or a multi-color pack
- Beading thread and needle
- Crimp beads
- Toggle clasp
- Pliers

What you'll do:

1. Determine how big you'd like the necklace to be. Roughly five strands will give you a necklace approximately 1-inch in diameter, but you can use more or fewer strands to vary the different looks.
2. Cut as many pieces of thread as you want your necklace to have strands. Each piece of thread should measure roughly 10-inches in length.
3. Tie a knot at the end of each one of the threads.

4. Begin placing seed beads on the threads. Seed beads are very small beads, and even those that come in solid colors will have some variation in color and size of bead. This is OK, and will lend some additional interest to the finished piece. If you are using multi-color seed beads, be sure to grab them at random to mix them evenly throughout the piece.

5. Completely cover each one of the threads with beads, leaving about 1-inch free at the end of each thread.

6. Gather up the strands in one hand and clip off their knots.

7. Slide a crimp bead over the strands, leaving it very close to the top.

8. Pass the ends of the thread through one end of a toggle clasp and back into the crimp bead, keeping the crimp as close to the toggle as you can. This will leave some space between the seed beads and the crimp.

9. Pinch the crimp closed with your pliers.

10. Turn the bead strands upside down and hold them by the knots so that the beads slide down against the crimp bead on the other end.

11. Hold tightly to the threads with one hand while you twist the beads around each other several times with your free hand. When you reach the desired amount of twists, slide a crimp bead over the loose threads, this time pushing it up tightly against the seed beads.

12. Pass the end of the threads through the other side of the toggle clasp and back into the crimp bead, pulling the loose ends very tight so that the crimp bead and clasp are right up against the seed beads on both ends of the necklace.

13. Pinch the crimp bead shut and clip off the excess threads.

14. Try on your necklace.

Floating Bead Necklace

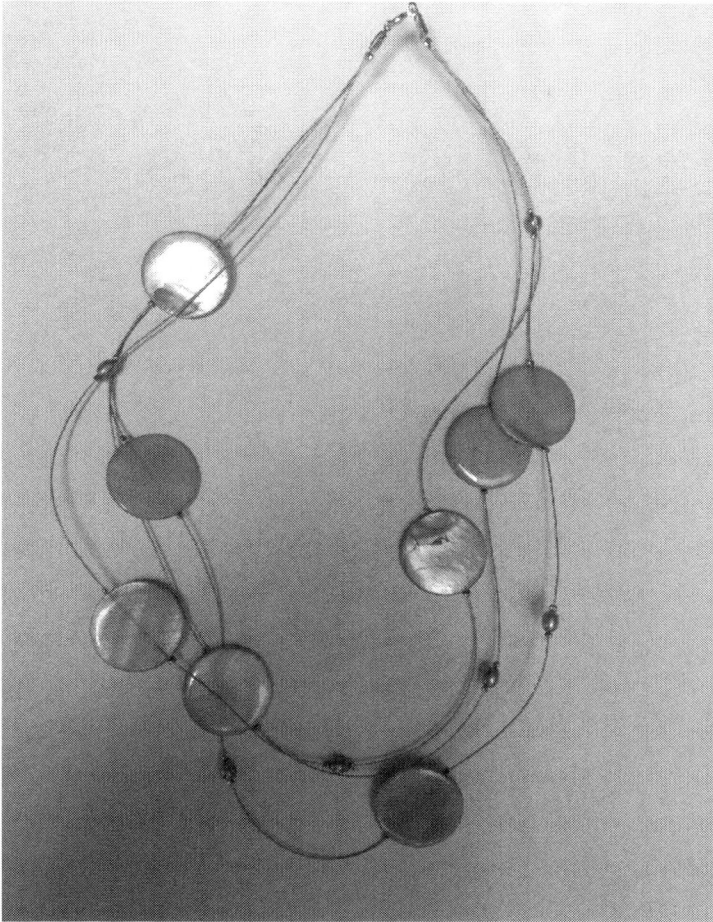

Negative space is one of the most important things to remember when designing jewelry; it has almost as big an impact as the areas you fill with beads. This floating bead necklace uses a lot of negative space around the mother of pearl discs and fresh water pearl beads. The effect is striking and elegant simply because of that old saying, "Less is more".

Floating bead necklaces can be elegant or fun depending on the colors you use and the beads you introduce on the strands. You can also use as many strands as you like to make the necklace more substantial or lighter, and you can also vary the length of your necklace as well.

I played around with a lot of materials when designing this necklace, and I found that the discs really help anchor the whole thing. Be sure that if you replace the discs with something else that you find something equally heavy, yet simple. The discs help give the necklace weight – something that it's lacking otherwise because of all the negative space. At the same time, the simplicity is what makes this necklace so perfect for an evening out or to layer on for a business meeting. Keeping the color of the discs and the beads similar helps to further the effect.

What you'll need:

- Woven metal wire
- Wire cutters
- Crimp beads
- Mother of pearl discs, pearl beads, or beads of your choice
- Pliers
- Jump ring

- Clasp

What to do:

1. Measure out three strands of woven metal wire. One should be approximately 14-inches, one 13-inches, and one 12-inches.

2. Take one strand of wire and slide a crimp bead about 2/3 of the way down.

3. Pinch the bead with pliers to hold it firmly in place on the wire.

4. Follow the crimp bead with a disc and a second crimp bead to hold the disc in place on the wire.

5. Slide a third crimp bead down so that it ends a few inches from the first and repeat. The idea is to place the beads at fairly random intervals on the three strands so that they do not overlap one another once the necklace is finished. Mix up the beads as you go, alternating discs and smaller beads.

6. Repeat with the two other strands, varying the distances and starting places of the beads until all three strands have discs floating at random intervals filling most of the space.

7. Gather together the three strands in one hand and pull them up together at the end.

8. Take the shortest wire and slide it up about ½-inch above the others and slide a crimp bead over the three strands. Do not pinch it shut.

9. Take a jump ring and thread the single strand that is longer than the others through the ring and back down into the crimp bead.

10. Pinch the crimp bead closed. This will join the three strands together with a jump ring at the end.

11. Gather the three strands on the other side and pull one strand higher than the others. Slide a crimp bead onto the three strands, but do not pinch.

12. Take a clasp and slide the single strand through the loop at the bottom of the clasp and thread it back down into the crimp bead.

13. Close the crimp bead. This will join the other side of the necklace and attach the clasp, which can now be connected to the jump ring to complete the necklace.

Wood and Blister Pearl Necklace

This fun and flirty necklace is filled with character, texture, and color. It's made of wooden beads you make yourself held together with jump rings and wire, rather than traditional materials. You can vary the colors, sizes of the beads, and the materials you mix with the wood to create a very creative and unique necklace that's perfect for an afternoon spent shopping with friends or for a girls' night out at a trendy wine and paint bar.

Because you're dictating the size of the wires and beads, you can also dictate how long or short the final necklace is. Just remember that wooden beads like this are extremely light; you'll need to have an anchor bead at the bottom to help the necklace hang right when it's finished. To vary the final effect, be sure to leave some of your wooden beads with the bark still on; it will give a deeper, darker tone beneath the paint. For a little extra sparkle, use an iridescent paint, or mix in an iridescent medium into the paint before you apply it.

What you'll need:

- Multiple wooden beads you've made from sticks, some with the bark on and some with the bark removed
- Blister pearls
- Ceramic or glass beads
- Paint
- Paintbrush
- 18 gauge wire
- Wire cutters
- Pliers

- Jump rings

What to do:

1. Paint your wooden beads so that they match the color of the blister pearls and other beads you're using in the necklace. Using a single color lets the texture of the various beads become the focal point of the piece. Let the beads dry completely after painting.
2. Cut a piece of wire to about 2-inches in length.
3. Bend one end of the wire into a small loop that is large enough to accommodate a jump ring.
4. Thread a wooden bead onto the wire and close the other end into a loop.
5. Attach a jump ring onto either loop.
6. Bend the end of a second wire into a loop, attaching it to one of the jump rings you've attached to the other wire.
7. Thread a blister pearl onto the open end of the wire and close it into a loop.
8. Attach a jump ring to the loop.
9. Bend a third wire into a loop, attach it to the others with a jump ring, and add a wooden bead.

10. Repeat but with a glass or ceramic bead.

11. Continue this pattern until you form a long chain and attach the ends together at the top.

12. Make a short chain of about 3-inches in length ending with a blister pearl to give it some weight and attach it to the center of the long chain to pull it down slightly to finish.

Lapis and Mother of Pearl Wire Necklace

Sometimes the jewelry that you wear to the office needs to be elegant, yet have a little edge to it to let your personality shine through. That's what this piece is all about; the mother of pearl and lapis lazuli beads scream culture, while the wire links that you put together yourself give it a little bit of an industrial or even steam punk feel. Remember that you can use any color of wire to boost the final effect; bright green would play beautifully off the blue beads, while sunny yellow could bring to mind a day at the beach.

While you can play with the length of this necklace somewhat – it would be stunning in a longer length – keep in mind that the beads and wire do have a tendency to get very heavy and if you're planning on wearing it for a full day of work at the office that it can lead to a little neck strain over time. Keeping it hitting in mid-chest will allow you to wear it comfortably all day.

What you'll need:

- 18 gauge wire
- ½-inch lapis lazuli beads
- 1/8-inch mother of pearl beads
- Wire cutters
- Pliers

What to do:

1. Cut a piece of wire to about 1-1/2-inches in length.
2. Bend one end of the wire into an elongated loop.
3. Thread a piece of lapis lazuli onto the open end of the wire and close it into another loop.

4. Repeat with a piece of mother of pearl, and thread the first loop through one of the loops on the lapis so that the two are joined with two loops between the two beads.

5. Continue alternating lapis and mother of pearl for approximately 26 beads in all.

6. Reopen the ends of the wire on either end of the necklace, and thread the open ends through each side of the loop on a clasp. Close the loops back up to complete the necklace.

Bracelet Designs

Bracelets tend to come and go in fashion. Once upon a time, many sweater makers actually ended the sleeves of their creations slightly short at what was known as "bracelet length" so that the wearer could show off whatever they were wearing on their wrists.

Not as flashy or obvious as a necklace or a pair of earrings, bracelets are more subtle in their design and use. Unless you're wearing a large cuff, or a number of bangles together, a bracelet may go unnoticed or overlooked depending on what you're wearing.

In the summer, however, when arms are bare, bracelets make the perfect accessory. They're also a great addition for people that like to talk with their hands, because the bracelet gets a lot of prominent placement this way.

These bracelet designs are meant to be worn in all kinds of occasions, whether you want to bare your arms or you just want a subtle clinking at your wrist to draw the gaze. Feel free to change up the colors and materials to help call as much attention to them as you like.

Metal Twist Bangle

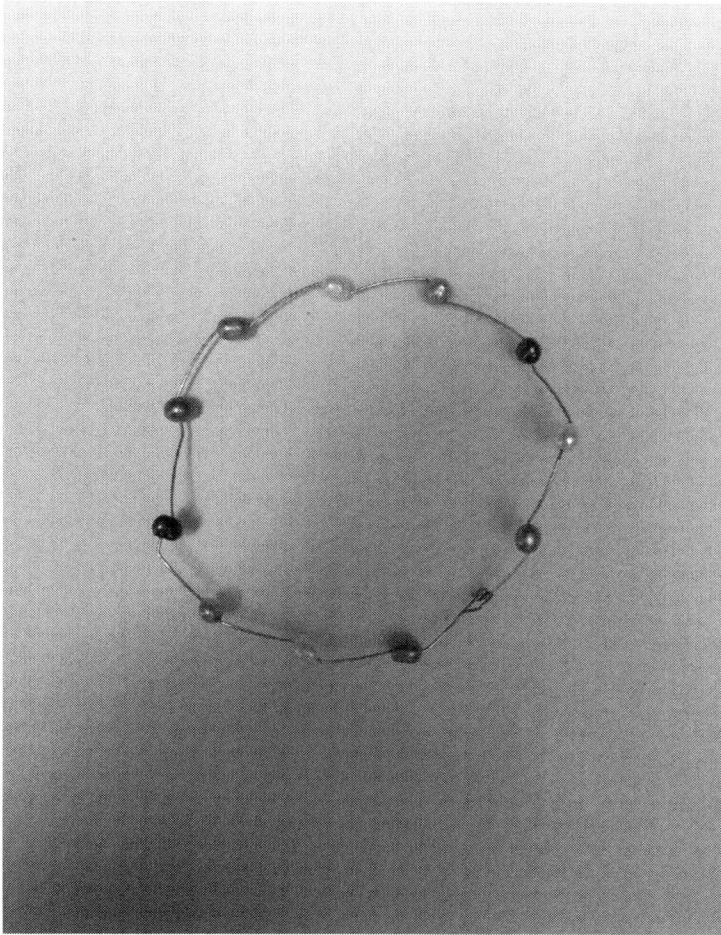

This is a very simple bangle that's a great project for intermediate beaders, and those that are interested in the ideas of combining color patterns with negative space. You only need two materials to make it – wire and beads – the combinations of how you put it together can be nearly endless. I like to play around with different color combinations using this bangle because it gives you the chance to see how colors work together with space between them, rather than pushing them against one another, which can sometimes be harder to judge. You can use any material, but I find that pearls and natural stone beads in similar sizes add a lot of depth to the finished design. Be sure not to use beads larger than 1/8-inch, or they'll overwhelm the finished bracelet.

These lightweight bangles are also a lot of fun to layer together on your arm, and they won't weigh you down over time either, so they're great for a day at the office or a day at the park chasing your kids. It's easy to size the bracelet so that it slides on and off without a clasp, so you can put these together in just minutes – hand them out as party favors at your next get together or tuck them inside of larger gifts for friends. These versatile bangles are always a huge hit.

What you'll need:

- 18 gauge wire
- Pliers
- Assortment of colored beads

What to do:

1. Measure out enough wire to comfortably go around your wrist, sliding over your hand. Make sure to make this piece of wire a little longer than you would ordinarily, because the twisting will shorten it slightly.

2. Measure a short ways up the wire and twist the wire about ¾ of the way around using the pliers.

3. Slide a bead up the wire until you reach the twist, then twist the wire on the other side another ¾.

4. Repeat at even intervals around the bracelet until each one of the beads is held firmly in place on either side by the twists.

5. Finish off the bracelet by overlapping the two ends a small amount and twisting the wire ends securely around one another to hold them closed.

Beaded Charm Bracelet

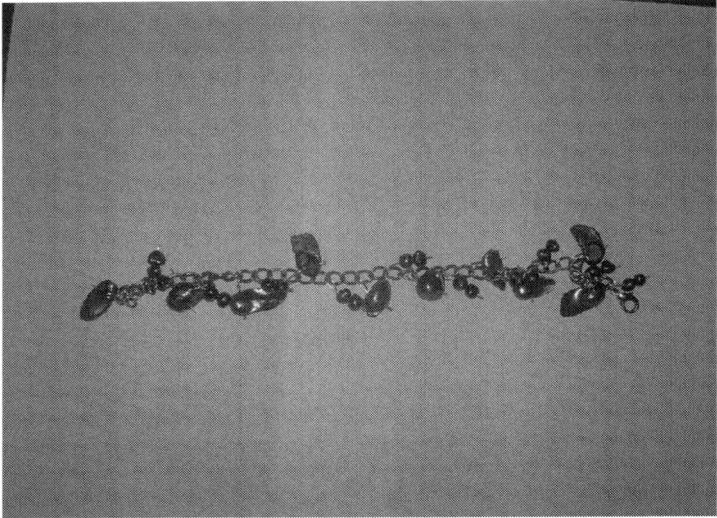

Remember the charm bracelets you had as a kid? This grown-up version uses a combination of pearls and previous stone beads for an elegant, yet playful design that you can wear to the office each day.

The chain itself can be made up of jump rings if you want to make the whole thing yourself, or you can use any simple bracelet chain in any finish. Just be sure that the links are large enough to comfortably thread a wire through, and that the chain has a clasp on the ends to make it easy to put on and take off.

I've made numerous charm bracelets in this style, changing up the colors of the beads and the materials. I really like the look of blister pearls and fresh water pearls that have been dyed rich colors. A blister pearl has a little of the mother of pearl from the shell still attached to it, which makes gives it an irregular appearance. I like to pair them up with fresh water pearls of the same color to add some extra interest and depth to the design. And if you feel like getting more playful and working in a charm or two into the design, just replace the beads and have some fun with the finished bracelet.

What you'll need:

- Bracelet chain
- 20 gauge wire
- Pliers
- Wire cutters
- Assorted beads

What to do:

1. Determine how many "charms" you want hanging off of the bracelet. Each charm can consist of one larger bead or several smaller beads – at this point you just need to know how many you'll place on the links. Most chains work best with a charm every other link so they don't get too crowded, but depending on the size of your links, you may want to insert one every link.

2. Measure out a piece of 20 gauge wire to about 1-inch in length and cut it. Repeat for as many charms as you intend to hang from the bracelet.

3. Grasp a piece of wire firmly in one hand.

4. Hold the pliers in the other hand and take hold of the very tip of the wire.

5. Bend the tip of the wire over into a loop. You want these loops to be very small, just larger than the hole in your beads to stop the beads from running off the ends.

6. Repeat for the rest of the pieces of wire.

7. Take a piece of wire and hold it with the loop down. Slide your bead or beads onto the wire so they stop at the loop.

8. Thread the other end of the wire through one of the links on the chain and bend the end of the wire so it doubles back down on itself. Depending on the size of the bead or beads you are using, you may need to trim away some excess wire at this time. You want to have the beads dangling slightly from the chain on a short piece of wire.

9. Take the remaining wire after cutting and loop it through the chain link a second time, wrapping it over the link so it holds on securely.

10. Repeat for the rest of the pieces of wire and beads for the bracelet.

Multi-Strand Stone Bracelet

This is a fun bracelet designed to catch the eye and get a little attention. Unlike cuff bracelets or coil bracelets, this is made up of individual strands joined together at the clasp. You can mix sizes of stone within it to help give it a different feel, as well as change the number of strands that you use throughout it. Some stones are also available in a variety of shapes. This multi-colored stone pictured comes in both round beads and chips, by mixing them together, you can get a lot of dimension to the finished piece.

Natural stones like granite or marble make some of the best beads for this type of bracelet. This is because no two stone beads will ever look exactly the same. Looking for a stone that can range from green to red to gold or that has a lot of veining and natural variation can really spice up the finished piece. This way, even though you're only using one "color" of bead, you can get a lot of dimension out of the finished piece.

Another thing that helps give this bracelet some interest is the use of negative space. This means that instead of stringing beads constantly along each of the wires, you'll leave some random gaps in the design. This helps prevent the finished piece from both getting too busy and too heavy. You can vary the number and the size of the gaps, just be sure that you place them in different spots on the three strands so that they don't overlap with one another. You can also leave gaps on only one or two strands to vary the final design as well.

What you'll need:

- Memory wire
- Crimp beads
- Stone beads in at least two sizes

- Large clasp
- Pliers
- Wire cutters

What you'll do:

1. Measure out two pieces of memory wire measuring about 5-inches long each, and one measuring 6-inches. If you like, you can vary the lengths of each piece slightly to make the bracelet look a little funkier when complete.

2. Line up the three pieces of memory wire and slip a crimp bead over one end. Make sure the one that is slightly longer sticks out past the others by about ½-inch. Pass the longer piece of wire through the end of a clasp and back into the crimp bead.

3. Squeeze the bead shut to hold the three pieces of wire together with one half of the clasp attached to the end.

4. Pour out your beads into a small bowl or bag and mix them together. This will enable you to grab different sizes of beads randomly. Or, if you prefer, you can make each strand of wire a different size of bead to mix things up that way.

5. Thread the stone beads onto the wires. The idea is to make sure that you get an even mix of color and size in the stones throughout the three wires. This will give you some variation in the finished piece.

6. Make a gap in your beads by sliding a crimp bead down the wire until it reaches the last bead threaded.

7. Push the crimp bead up tightly against the other beads and squeeze it shut.

8. Slide a second crimp bead down the wire, but stop this one a little way up the wire so that you leave some negative space in the final design.

9. Squeeze the crimp bead shut and continue sliding more beads onto the wire. You can make as many gaps as you want, and make them as large or small as you want to vary the final design.

10. Repeat for the other two strands.

11. Pinch the ends of the three wires together. One wire will stick out longer than the others by about ½-inch.

12. Slide a crimp bead down the wires until it touches the stones. Pass the longer wire through the other

end of the clasp and back down into the crimp
bead.

13. Squeeze the bead shut.

14. Trim off any excess wires extending out past the
crimp bead on either end to avoid any snags.

15. Try on your new bracelet.

Ellen Warren

Bird's Nest Bracelet

For mother's that love the bird's nest design of the pendent, this bracelet is designed to match and complement the look. Rather than a single nest, however, this bracelet is made up of multiple nests joined together by jump rings. I like to use nests of two different colors to mix up the design a little, but you can use nests of a solid color or mix up the colors within each nest to get the desired look.

The end result is a little reminiscent of a charm bracelet. The way that it moves, however, will make you think of links in a chain. While simple in its execution, this bracelet is extremely eye catching; the way that the light hits the individual links will draw the eye of anyone nearby.

You can easily change the size of this bracelet by adding or subtracting a nest. I suggest making it slowly, and trying it on a few times as you go until you get the perfect fit. It's meant to be loose, but not so loose that it slides down off your hand when the clasp is done.

Like the bird's nest pendent, you can use any material for the nests, but I find that pearls and semi-precious stones make the best eggs for their color and luminescence. If you like, you can also use colored wire to surround the eggs, changing up the look completely by surrounding your eggs in copper or bronze colored wire, which will make the lighter colored eggs really pop inside.

What you'll need:

18 gauge silver-plated wire

- Multiple beads measuring about 1/8-inch in diameter
- Pliers
- Wire cutters

- Jump Rings
- Bracelet clasp

What you'll do:

1. Make your first nest. I find that when making multiple nests like these that it's easiest to do things in stages. Make all your nests, then wire all your eggs in, and finally attach all the nests together to form the bracelet.

2. Wrap a piece of wire around your index finger roughly 20 times to form the outside of the nest.

3. Change its final side by pulling on the loose ends of the wire to tighten the nest and make it smaller, or by placing a pair of pliers in the center of the nest and opening them outward to make it larger.

4. Cut a small piece of wire, about ½-inch long and wrap it around the side of the nest to hold it securely in place.

5. Repeat for roughly 10 nests.

6. Cut a piece of wire about 4-inches long to thread your beads together to form the eggs.

7. Slide three beads onto the wire so they stop in the center.

8. Bend the wire upward so that the three eggs form a triangle at the bottom of the wire.

9. Cross the two long ends of the wire over each other and pull them down the sides of the triangle.

10. Place the eggs in the center of a nest and wrap the two long ends around the nest on either side to hold the eggs securely in place. As you do this, leave one loop higher than the others on either side; this is where you will attach the jump rings that hold the bracelet together. Make sure that these two loops are directly opposite each other on either side of the nest.

11. Repeat for the remaining nests.

12. Take a nest and a jump ring. Open the jump ring and thread it through one of the open loops on either side of the nest. Attach a second jump ring to the loop on the other side.

13. Open up the second jump ring a second time, this time attaching it to one of the open loops on a second nest. This will link the two nests together.

14. Take a third jump ring and attach it to the other side of the second nest.

15. Repeat until you have joined together all of your nests into a straight row.
16. Attach one side of a clasp to the first jump ring you attached to the first nest.
17. Attach the other side of the clasp to the last jump ring you attached to the last nest.
18. Piece together the two ends of the clasp to close the bracelet, and try it on.

Simple Stones Bracelet

Sometimes all your outfit needs is a little bit of color to help brighten it up. If you're at the office or someplace formal for the evening, you don't want this to be a big, chunky piece that will overwhelm your outfit, just give it a bit of a pick-me-up. That's what this simple stone bracelet is made to do; add a little bit of color and life to whatever you're wearing, without necessarily detracting attention away from it.

This is a very simple and easy bracelet to make. What gives it its charm is the use of clear and iridescent materials. I like to use a mix of semi-precious stones that are translucent like quartz and amethyst, and mix these with some natural and blister pearls. The contrast of the opaque but luminescent pearls with the translucent stones brings a lot of depth to the bracelet. By using colors that are all analogous to one another – meaning that they all sit beside one another on the color wheel – you can use a lot of different color variations that will still have a very subtle look to them. This makes the finished piece perfect for pairing with nearly anything that just needs a little color to help set it off and make it complete.

What you'll need:

- Memory wire
- Mix of beads all the same size – look for quartz, pearls, and even sea glass that are similar in color
- Crimp beads
- Pliers
- Wire cutters
- Bracelet clasp

What you'll do:

1. Cut a length of memory wire just big enough to go around your wrist, while allowing two fingers to slip in beneath it. You want this to be close fitting, but not snug when it's complete.

2. Slide a crimp bead down one side just slightly, then pass the end of that wire through the loop on one piece of the clasp.

3. Thread the wire back into the crimp bead and press the bead tightly closed with your pliers to hold the wire in place with the clasp caught in the loop at the end.

4. Take the time to arrange your beads by color. You may want to set up a pattern at this point, such as pink, gold, purple, white, pink. Play around with the colors until you find a pattern that looks natural and subtle, but that pulls together nicely.

5. Begin threading your beads onto the memory wire in the pattern you determined. Stop when you have about ½-inch of wire left on the end.

6. Slide a crimp bead down onto the wire, pressing it right up against the beads.

7. Pass the open end of the wire through the other side of the clasp and push it back down into the crimp bead.

8. Press the crimp bead tightly closed with the pliers to secure the clasp in a loop at the end of the bracelet.

9. Try it on.

Multiple Twisted Bangles

Going for a funky or eclectic look with your bracelets doesn't mean that you need to go heavy or chunky as well. You can get a fun, flirty look using some very thin wire bangles as well. This bracelet takes a basic wire bangle design, and puts several of them together joined with a large bead at the top. The effect has a lot of color and interest, but is extremely lightweight and airy at the same time.

If you like, you can also keep each one of the bangles separate from one another and simply wear them all loose at once. This way they'll tinkle together as you move and draw additional attention to them.

You can use any kind of beads for these bangles, but you'll want to keep them small and all roughly the same size. If you go too big, the bangles won't hang together properly and the finished piece might become too heavy to wear.

I like to use a variety of colors on each bangle, and to vary the placement of each color each time around. This helps give the finished bracelet a kaleidoscope effect, as if the bangles and colors are spinning on your arm.

You can use as few or as many strands in this bracelet as you like. I recommend at least three to give it enough movement and play, but you can piece together five or six easily as well. Too many does get difficult to join at the top, however, so you may need to either make two or three complete bracelets to wear together, or to simply wear them loose if you want to use more than that at a time.

What you'll need:

- 20 gauge-silver plated wire
- Pliers

- Wire cutters
- Large bead that has a wide opening – at least ¼-inch
- Multiple small beads in a variety of colors, measuring approximately 1/8-inch

What you'll do:

1. Cut as many pieces of wire as you want your finished bracelet to have loops. Each piece should be roughly 5-inches in length. You can vary the size depending on the size of your hand and wrist; there is no clasp so the finished bracelet needs to be able to slip over your hand, yet stay in place and not slip off once on.

2. Pick up your first wire and bend a small twist into it about 1-inch from the end.

3. Slide a bead onto the wire until it reaches this twist and stops. Make another twist on the other side of the bead to hold it in place on the wire.

4. Make a third twist about 1-inch down the bracelet from where the first bead sits. Slide down another bead and twist the other side to hold it.

5. Repeat until you have about 4 to 5 beads on the wire, then repeat with the other wires.

6. Gather up all of your wires together.

7. Bend them into a circle and slide your large bead onto one end of the wires.

8. Slide the other end of the wires into the large bead.

9. Push the bead slightly to one side so that you can see the ends of both sides of the wires.

10. Twist these together tightly so that the bangles fan out away from one another.

11. Slide the large bead back over the twists to hide them, and bend the ends of the wire down just slightly on either side to hold the bead in place.

12. Try on your new bracelet.

Three Strand, Three Color Bracelet

This bracelet is meant to bridge the gap between the multi-strand stone bracelet and the simple stone bracelet. Meaning that sometimes you need a little more color and variation than the multi-strand bracelet, which uses one stone can give you, but you want something a little beefier than the single strand of the simple stone bracelet.

This bracelet uses three separate strands of beads, each with its own color. The trick, however, is that the beads don't completely cover each of the strands. They float along the wires using crimp beads to help hold them in place. So you get an elegant, simplistic bracelet that also has a degree of complexity to it.

You can choose analogous colors for this bracelet as well, sticking with shades that are subtly different from one another, or you can use more complementary colors that can give you a bolder look. Because there's lots of visual blanks space in the finished piece, even very bold, vivid, or contrasting colors won't overwhelm the finished design. This makes it the perfect bracelet to wear to the office or for an evening out; depending on what other accessories or outfits you pair it with, this bracelet can take on a lot of different personas.

What you'll need:

- Memory wire
- Crimp beads
- Bracelet clasp
- Pliers
- Wire cutters
- Three colors of beads, all roughly the same size and shape

What you'll do:

1. Cut two strands of memory wire about 5-inches in length, and one strand 6-inches in length.

2. Hold the three strands together so that the long piece sticks out evenly past the others on either side.

3. Slide a crimp bead onto the three strands on one end.

4. Pass the long end of the single wire through one end of a clasp and back down into the crimp bead, so that the clasp hangs from a loop. Squeeze the crimp bead shut with your pliers to hold it tight.

5. Take another crimp bead and slide it down one of the three strands, stopping anywhere you like.

6. Squeeze the bead shut so that it stays put on the strand.

7. Slide a bead on after it, followed by another crimp bead. This will freeze the bead on the wire.

8. Repeat with more crimp beads and colored beads on this strand until you have the desired amount.

9. Repeat using other colors on the two other strands. Be sure to move the position of each bead along the

strand so that they don't touch each other when the three strands are lined up.

10. Hold the ends of the three strands together once you've finished beading them. The longest piece should stick out about ½-inch past the others.

11. Slide a crimp bead onto the three strands, then push the long wire through the other end of a clasp and back into the crimp bead.

12. Squeeze the bead tightly to hold the toggle in place and secure the three wires together.

13. Try on your new bracelet.

Earring Designs

There's nothing quite like a good pair of earrings for drawing attention to your face and adding a little pizzazz to your outfit. Earrings are one of the most versatile forms of jewelry. Yes, necklaces can be long or short and bracelets and rings can be chunky or thin, but earrings really run the gamut of styles. You can have subtle, classic little studs or giant dangling earrings that touch your shoulders.

Earrings can be made to move when you do, swinging gently to further draw attention to them, or they can remain quietly hidden beneath your hair, only peeking out once in a while. Best of all, there is an earring for every occasion and situation. While some events may make wearing a long necklace or bracelet difficult, a good pair of studs or some mildly dangling earrings are still usually a sure bet.

Like other forms of jewelry, you can make earrings out of nearly anything. In fact, you actually have a little more versatility with earrings than you do with other forms of jewelry, because some types of earrings can be positioned so that you only see one side. I once made a bunch of earrings out of ShrinkyDinks – this just wouldn't work quite the same way on a necklace!

These earring designs are meant to both match some of the necklace and bracelet designs already listed. Others are designed to stand on their own. Like the other pieces in this book, feel free to change up the colors or materials, as well as the basic size of each piece until you get exactly what you're looking for.

Earrings are one of the most playful and fun types of jewelry to make, so be sure to have a little fun and take a walk on the wild side with some of your materials and color selections.

Bird's Nest Earrings

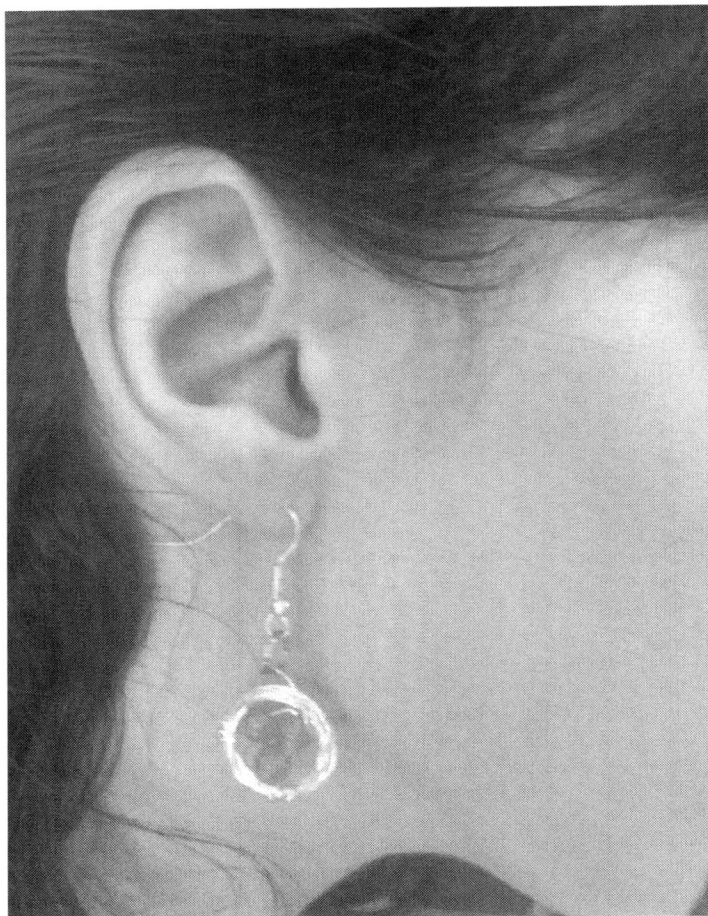

Meant to match the pendant and bracelet made with bird's nests, these dangling earrings are subtle enough to be worn every day, but eye catching enough to garner a little attention. Each nest measures around 5/8-inch when complete, and dangles from a jump ring hooked onto a standard earring wire. So they'll move just a bit when you turn your head, but you won't find them getting caught in your hair.

Because you have two earrings to a set, feel free to change up the colors between them. For example, if you have two children make a nest using a color that symbolizes each one. Or just have fun and find some stones for the centers that can make some colorful and eye catching eggs.

What you'll need:

- 20-gauge silver-plated wire
- Pliers
- Wire cutters
- 6 small beads all measuring roughly 1/8-inch in size
- Two jump rings
- Two earring wires

What you'll do:

1. Wrap a piece of silver wire around your index finger about 20 times to form the basic form of the nest.

2. Clip off the excess wire, and tighten up the nest by taking the two loose ends and pulling them tight. If you tighten the nest too much, open it back up by

inserting your pliers into the center of nest and opening them up to push it back open.

3. Cut a piece of wire about ½-inch long and wrap it around one edge of the nest to hold its shape.

4. Cut another piece of wire roughly 4-inches long.

5. Slide three beads onto the wire, stopping them when they reach the center.

6. Bend the two sides of the wire up so that the beads form a triangle shape in the center.

7. Cross the wires over one another and pull them down the sides of the triangle so that they angle off the bottom.

8. Place the beads in the center of the nest and use the two long, open pieces of wire to wrap around the nest to secure the beads in place.

9. Leave one of the loops of wire slightly open and taller than the others. This is where you'll attach the jump ring to put the earring together.

10. Open up a jump ring and thread it through the loop on the nest.

11. Thread the jump ring through the loop at the bottom of an earring wire. If your earring wire is slightly open at the bottom of the loop, use your

pliers to open it wide enough to insert the jump ring easily, then pinch it closed again to hold it securely.

12. Repeat for the other earring.

13. Try them on.

Feather Earrings

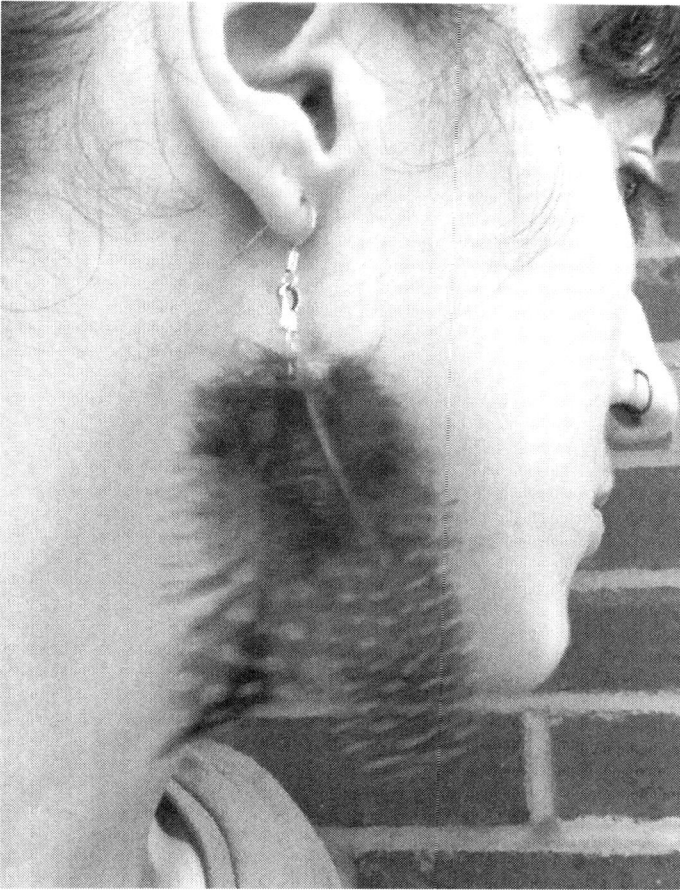

Going out clubbing or dancing calls for some really unusual and funky jewelry. But a lot of dancing and movement can make heavy earrings feel like they weigh a hundred pounds by the end of the night. That's why these feather earrings are so great; they're super lightweight so they won't weigh you down, but they're long enough and bright enough that they're sure to catch everyone's attention.

Feathers that are all in one piece, and not made up of multiple strands also won't get caught in your hair, so you can dance, twirl, and party the night away without worrying about getting tangled up over time. You can also find feathers in a wide assortment of different colors and textures. So play around with some fluffy neon feathers, then go for some sleeker feathers with a black outline around the solid interior.

You'll need to use at least one bead at the top of each earring to help them hang properly from the earring wire. You can choose to blend this bead in by picking one in a similar color to the feathers, or choose something that will stand out and become part of the overall design. Either way, these lightweight feathers are sure to get a lot of attention.

What you'll need:

- Two earring wires
- Two long crimp beads
- 18-gauge wire

- Two beads of your choice
- Two to four feathers of your choice

What'll you'll do:

1. Select your feather and bead combinations. Depending on the feathers that you use, you may need more than one per earring to flesh it out a little.

2. Cut a piece of wire about 1-inch in length. You may end up trimming this down later, but it's better to have too much than not enough when you get started.

3. Bend the wire slightly and put it through the loop at the bottom of the earring wire. Continue bending the wire until it forms a loop joining the wire to the earring wire.

4. Slide the bead of your choice onto the wire.

5. Slide a long crimp bead onto the wire after the bead.

6. Tuck the stem of the feather of feathers up into the crimp bead along with the wire itself. When the feathers are securely fastened, pinch the crimp bead shut to hold them in place.

7. Trim away the excess wire from below the crimp bead so that it stays flush with the bottom of the bead.

8. Fluff up the feathers, bending them out of the wire slightly so that they take up a little extra space.

9. Try on your new earrings.

Dangling Charm Earrings

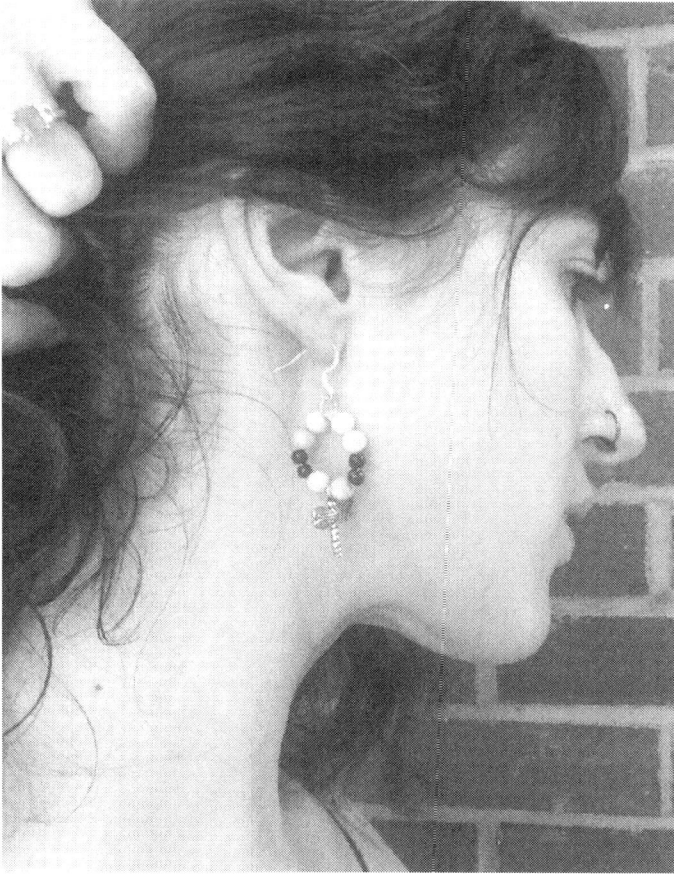

Sometimes you want an earring that will move a little, remain lightweight enough to wear for a while, but not necessarily gather a lot of attention. These beaded charm earrings are meant to do just that. They form a circle of beads that a charm can hang from, either from the top so that the charm sits in the center of the circle, or from the bottom of the circle to weigh it down and give it a little shape.

The best part of this design is that you can use anything at all for the charm. Choose a gorgeous Swarovski crystal to catch the light, or choose a novelty charm to add a little bit of fun and whimsy to an outfit. You can also coordinate the beads that form the circle of the earring with the charm below so that the charm either stands out more, or forms a more subtle effect.

The overall earring is fairly lightweight because the center of the beads remain open. Therefore, you can enlarge the overall design to make some larger earrings that dangle the charm from the top to really catch the eye, or you can stick with the smaller design that will just add a little playful and colorful touch to any evening out.

I suggest using small beads – about 1/16-inch in size to keep the earring light. You can make the charm a little larger so that it becomes the focus of the piece. I like to use a mix of light and dark colors to add some depth to the overall design, but you can use a single color throughout the piece if you want to make it a little more subtle.

What you'll need:

Earring wires

- 20-gauge silver-plated wire
- Pliers

- Wire cutters
- Small beads of your choice of color
- Charm that has a loop at the top for attaching

What you'll do:

1. Cut a piece of wire to about 2-inches in length.
2. Bend the wire into roughly the shape of a circle. Take a look at the size of the circle; if you want your earrings to be smaller, clip the wire now. For larger earrings, cut your initial piece of wire longer.
3. Bend the very tip of one end of the wire into a small loop. This will help the beads stay in place while you add them to the wire. You will unbend the tip to attach it to the earring wire, so don't make the loop too small or tight.
4. Begin threading beads onto the wire. When you reach the halfway point in the wire, thread your charm on, then finish with the other beads. If you want your charm to be dangling from the bottom, you will close your loop and attach it to the earring wire on the other end. If you want your charm to inside the loop, you'll flip it upside down, twist the ends of the wire together and tuck them under a

bead to hide them, then attach the earring wire just to the side of the charm.

5. Attach your earring wire to the beaded loop. With your charm at the bottom, open up the small loop you made on one end, then pass both ends through the loop on the earring wire before bending them backwards to secure the loop into place.

6. Repeat for the other earring.

7. Try on your new dangling charm hoops.

Wire-Wrapped Circles

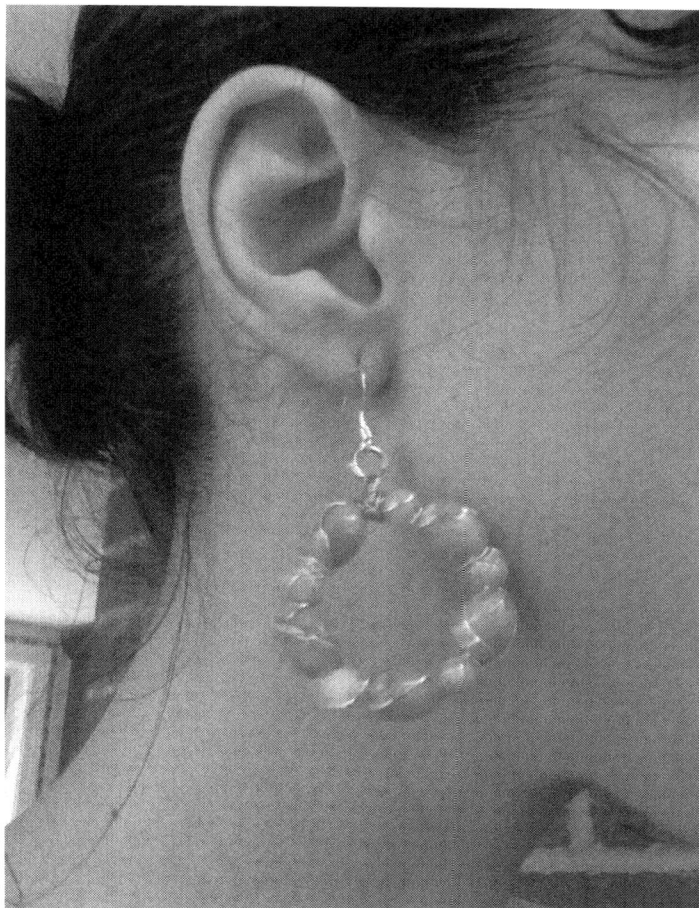

If you're looking for something that's colorful and fun, yet tasteful enough to wear to the office, these wire-wrapped circle earrings can do the trick. You can make them out of any two sizes of bead that are similar in color. The subtle variation of color and size adds a lot of depth to the finished design. The wire wrapping around the finished circles adds additional interest to the finished piece and sets them apart from simple beaded earrings.

I like to make these about 1-1/2-inches in diameter – just large enough to be seen and add some color to your face, but not so big that they get too heavy over the course of the day. You can, of course, change the size, making them larger or smaller. To keep them from getting too heavy, I suggest making sure that your beads are fairly lightweight. Ceramic beads that are very thin tend to work well for this; stone and glass tend to be thicker and therefore will weigh down a little harder on your ears over time.

If you're able to, try to use beads that are different shapes as well as different sizes. This helps the earrings to move a bit more and take on a little extra dimension. I like oblong beads for this piece because I think it helps make the circles seem a little larger than they really are when you're done.

What you'll need:

- 18-gauge silver plated wire
- Earring wires
- Two sizes of beads in similar colors
- Two jump rings
- Wire cutters
- Pliers

What you'll do:

1. Cut a piece of wire to about 7-inches in length.

2. Bend one end of the wire with your pliers into a small loop. You want this loop to be large enough to pass another wire through, and also to stop the beads from sliding off the end.

3. Begin beading your wire, alternating large and small beads until when you form the beaded part of the wire into a circle it measures about 1-1/2-inches in diameter with a long piece of wire left over.

4. Pass the open end of the wire through the loop you made at the beginning and pull. This will form your beads into a circle.

5. Take the long end of the wire that is leftover from the circle and begin wrapping it around the beads. Make a figure-eight pattern with the wire as you wrap to circle the beads from different angles.

6. Continue wrapping until you reach the top of the beaded circle again. Wrap the remaining wire around the top to form a small loop.

7. Attach a jump ring to the small loop, and the jump ring to the earring wire.

8. Repeat for the other earring.

9. Try them on.

Beaded Loops

Really big loop earrings are a lot of fun to wear, but they can be boring after a while when they're made of just simple metal. By making some big loop earrings and covering them with seed beads, you can add a little color, glitter, and interest to the same earrings. Best of all, seed beads are so lightweight, they won't weigh down the hoops making them difficult to wear.

By making your own hoops, you get to control how big they'll be. Want them to touch your shoulders? Or do you want them to just dip to the length of your chin? You're totally in control when you make your own beaded loops. You can also control the colors that go into them, such as using iridescent beads to make them sparkle or creating a rainbow by layering colors around the loop as you go.

Beaded loops are a lot of fun both to make and to wear. Once you make one pair, you may not be able to stop until you've made a set for every occasion imaginable.

What you'll need:

- 16-gauge silver plated wire
- Seed beads in your choice of color
- Pliers
- Wire cutters
- Earring wires

What you'll do:

1. Cut a length of wire to the size you want your finished earrings to be. You can bend the wire a little while it's still on the roll to help you figure out how big you'll want them to be. Take careful measurement of the final size so you can cut a second piece for the other earring.

2. Bend one end of the wire into a small loop, just large enough for another wire to pass through.

3. Begin threading seed beads onto the wire. You can use a single color, random colors, or make stripes and gradations.

4. Continue beading until you reach the other end of the wire.

5. Slip the open end of the wire through the loop, pulling it tight to form a circle.

6. Bend the open wire backwards over the top of the loop into a second loop to join the two ends.

7. Slip an earring wire loop through the joint of the two wire ends at the top of the earring.

8. Repeat for the other earring.

9. Try them on.

Wire Wrapped Column Earrings

These fun earrings can be made using a variety of different beads and colored wire to get personalized effects. A different variation on the wire-wrapped circles, these earrings use the same wire wrapping technique, but on a column of beads, rather than a loop. So while the technique is very similar, the effect is completely different, letting you mix and match several different bead and wire combinations to make a variety of earrings. You can also increase or shorten the length of the earrings by adding more or fewer beads to the final strand, and you can use more or fewer strands of wire to wrap them to get a variety of different looks. Remember that wire comes in a whole rainbow of colors; don't feel as though you need to stay with traditional silver-plated if you want to make something funky to wear out to the club at night. On the other hand, using silver-plated wire and mixing it with semi-precious stones can give you a pair of earrings that's perfect for wearing to the office each day.

I like the way that ceramic and glass stones mix here with the silver wire. The translucency of the glass along with the opaque ceramic beads and the shining wire give a lot of unexpected depth to the finished piece. Consider mixing a variety of different beads together to create a look that's unique to your tastes.

What you'll need:

- Two earring wires
- Glass or stone beads of your choice
- 20 gauge wire in a color of your choice
- Pliers
- Wire cutters

What to do:

1. Cut two strands of wire approximately 5 to 6-inches in length.

2. Hold the two wires together tightly in one hand; you will be threading the beads onto both wires at once.

3. Thread the beads onto the wires in the pattern you desire until you reach approximately 2-inches in length. Take care not to slide the beads off the ends of the wires.

4. Slide the beads so that there is about 1-inch of wire on one end and 2-inches of wire on the other.

5. Hold the wires tightly together on the shorter end by placing your thumb and forefinger against the beads. This will prevent them from sliding off the end while you wrap.

6. Separate the two wires on the other end of the beads.

7. Wrap the wires one at a time around the beads in a figure 8 pattern until you reach the top.

8. Wrap the ends of the two wires securely around the wire at the top of the beads, holding the beads in place at both ends by the wire.

9. Take hold of an earring wire in one hand and the beaded earring end in another.

10. Slide the open end of the wire through the loop at the end of the earring wire.

11. Bend the wire down from the loop and wrap it around itself to secure the earring to the earring wire.

12. Repeat for the other earring.

Other Projects

One of the best things about beaded jewelry is that it doesn't have to be conventional or follow conventional rules. You can not only create unique necklaces, bracelets, and earrings, you can also use the same techniques to create personalized rings and a whole host of other things from beaded tassels to zipper pulls. Try on these other projects for size; they're the perfect jumping off point for a variety of other ideas.

Coil Seed Bead Ring

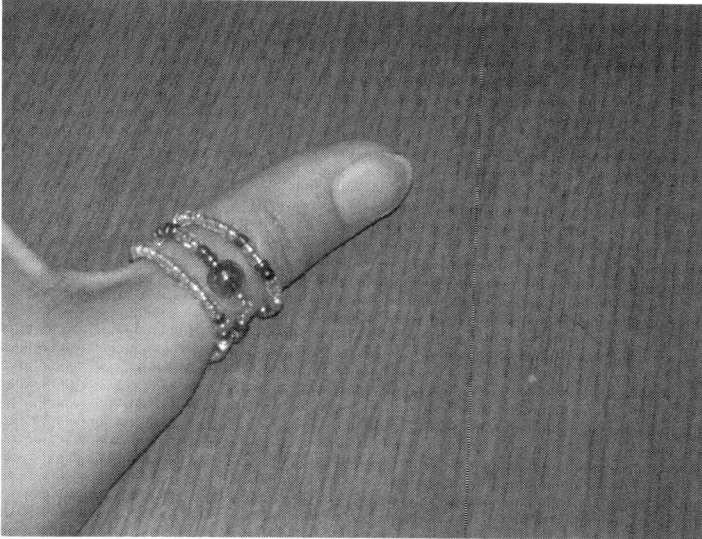

Get accustomed to working with seed beads before you start stitching by making this easy coil ring. Choose a mixture of seed beads that come in a variety of colors, and use them randomly over the ring to get a variegated look. This ring is adjustable and will fit any size finger once it's done.

What you'll need:

- 18 gauge wire
- Pliers
- Wire cutters
- Seed beads

- Larger glass bead

What to do:

1. Cut a piece of wire about 4-inches long.
2. Bend one end of the wire into a very small loop, just large enough to stop the seed beads from sliding off the end.
3. Begin threading seed beads onto the ring, mixing colors randomly until you reach the center of the wire. You can check this by matching up the two ends to one another and pulling down on the bottom of the wire.
4. Thread a larger glass bead onto the wire once you've covered half of it with seed beads.
5. Switch back to the seed beads and continue threading them onto the wire until you reach the end.
6. Twist the end of the wire into a small loop. If necessary, trim away any excess wire to ensure that the end loop is about the size of a seed bead so that it blends in with the finished ring.
7. Twist the ring into a coil to fit your finger by holding one end firmly and rotating the rest of the ring

140

around in a circle. The glass bead should sit in the center between two coils of seed beads. You can tighten the ring once it's on by pulling on the ends; loosen it by lifting up on the glass bead to uncoil the ring slightly, then let it go.

Coralling

Coralling is a more advanced beading technique that can be used to create all kinds of three dimensional jewelry. It's usually a technique that many people master before they move onto to stitching, and it can be used to create necklaces, bracelets, and earrings that have multiple components joined up together. You can use any size of bead, but the majority of coralling projects are done either with small beads or seed beads.

When you're beginning to coral, you may want to start with something abstract first. This is to get used to the technique of threading off several small branches that connect to the main trunk. Once you master this, you can start creating a lot of very intricate patterns; the key is just in how you go in and out of the branches.

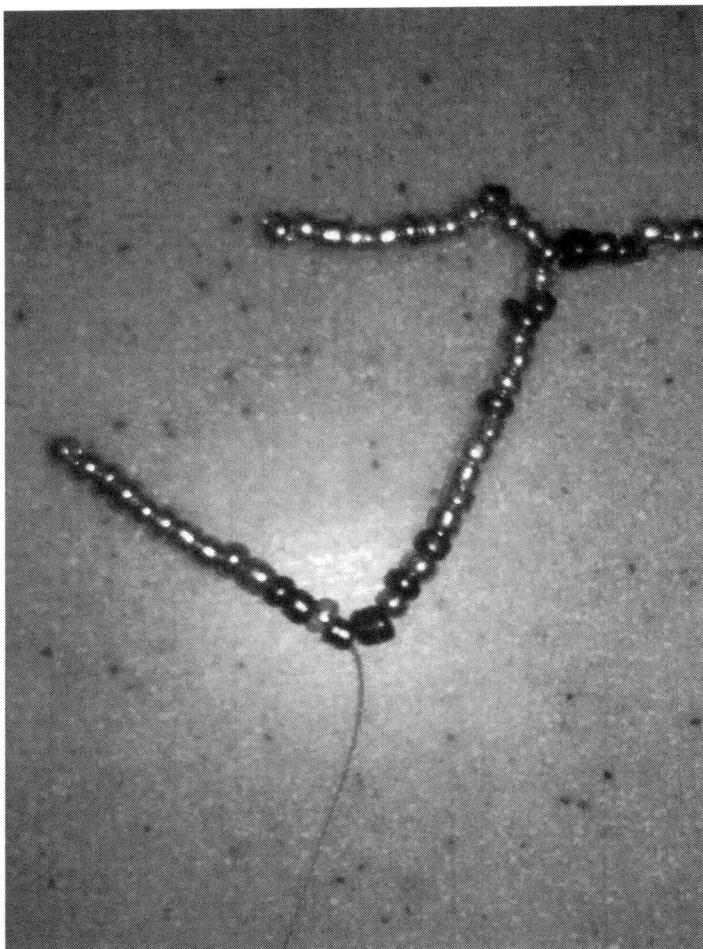

To learn how to coral properly, it's important to start with seed beads. Larger beads may seem easier to work with because they take up more space, but they can actually be more difficult to manipulate. Try this basic coralling technique using seed beads until you become comfortable. Then, you may want to try a simple project using larger beads, such as making a necklace that has several "branches" coming off of the main bib. Once you're comfortable with that, go ahead and start making some more intricate pieces. In time, you may find that stitching will give you the versatility you're looking for, and you'll be able to combine techniques to get the final look that you're after.

What you'll need:

- Thread – silk or very fine cotton – you may want to use a lot of thread on your first project so that you can practice multiple branches at once. If you want, start with a shorter piece of thread and just tie on more as you go to lengthen if you find that a single long thread is too cumbersome.
- Beading needle
- Seed beads

What to do:

1. Measure out a long piece of thread. You want to start with at least a foot, but you can start longer if you like.
2. Tie the beading needle to one end of the thread, and make a knot in the other end to stop the beads from slipping off the end.

3. Slide on as many seed beads as necessary to cover about 4-inches of the thread.

4. Pull the thread taut, go over the side of the last bead that you put on, and push your needle back into the row of beads one bead down from the top. This will securely hold your bead at the top in place, while creating a single beaded column or trunk.

5. Push your needle down a few beads, then have it exit out the side between two beads.

6. Begin sliding on more seed beads onto this new branch for about an inch or two. When you reach the end, repeat the method of working back down the same branch until you reach the trunk.

7. Go down the trunk two or three more beads, and make another branch coming out in another direction. You may want to make a few branches coming off of this secondary branch as well – think of the way that a tree has multiple branches or twigs.

8. Continue going up and down the trunk, making multiple branches and twigs until you feel comfortable with the technique. You should now have a piece of seed bead "coral", as well as the

rudimentary skills necessary to start stitching or creating some more intricate pieces of jewelry or bead art.

Shopping for Materials

There are two basic rules of thumb when shopping for materials to make your jewelry from: purchase things on an as-needed basis to get the exact pieces and colors you need at one time, or purchase items as they catch your fancy, having a large stockpile to go through when the time is right.

I recommend a mixture of both of these methods when you begin making your own beaded jewelry. Sometimes you really need a specific bead – either a special color, material, or size that you might not have purchased otherwise. On the other hand, if you pick things up wherever you go, you'll end up with a mixture of items that you might not have thought to put together previously.

I like to make crazy cuff bracelets, beaded snowflakes, and beaded flowers when I get down to just a few of a bunch of types of beads left in my supplies. Often the color and material combinations that I come up with for these pieces end up inspiring me to make something new using those colors and materials again later.

When you're shopping for materials and you come across something unusual or that really catches you fancy, be sure to write down all the info on its tag. This will help you find it again later, whether at the same store, a different one, or online. Many people often resell strings of beads on eBay, so if you run out of something and can't find a match at the location you originally bought it at, you may have luck hunting it down online if you have all the pertinent information. I know it can be tempting to rip off the tags and nylon and get to work with the beads, but by keeping any relevant info, you can be sure to find those specialty items again down the road.

Inspiration and Ideas

A lot of the pieces presented in this book were inspired by other things, places, people, and events. Sometimes it's the colors of a flower that I think work beautifully together and want to recreate, other times it's the feeling of something that I'm trying to capture.

Beaded jewelry is an art form like any other; your inspiration and ideas for color combinations or for unique pieces of your own can come from anywhere. Any of these projects can be used as a stepping off point for a variety of different projects all your own. All you have to do is start changing the colors, sizes, and materials and see where it takes you.

Once you start looking at the world with the eyes of an artist, you'll start finding inspiration everywhere you look. I've designed beaded pendants in the shape of owls, trees, and snowflakes. I've also made earrings that call to mind cherries on a stem and falling rain drops. Let the world be your style book, and you'll be creating beautiful pieces of jewelry that are all your own in no time. A few things that you may want to use to start getting inspiration from include:

Nature – look around at the colors and textures. You can also make your own beads out of pieces of quartz or beryls that you may find laying around. Small pieces of wood also make interesting beads if you drill through them lengthwise.

Other people's jewelry – sometimes you'll see a piece that catches your eye. Why not use it as a jumping off point for your own piece? Don't copy it exactly – let it inspire you. What was it you liked? The colors, textures, placement of the beads? Figure out what you like, then create your own piece based on those attributes. You'll be surprised when your finished piece looks very little like the one that inspired you in the first place, but still gives you those same kinds of thoughts.

Experiences – if you go away on vacation, on a hike, to a museum or anywhere that makes you feel something intense, try to capture that feeling in your jewelry. Think about the colors, scents, and textures that you saw while you were out, then look for beads that help recall those thoughts and feelings for you. Now think about where you were, and try to capture the style of the place – refined, earthy, sensual, etc. You'll quickly find that you're able to capture your experiences and thoughts in your art.

You can also use the pieces in this book as a way to jumpstart your own creativity. Start with small variations, or consider what it is about each piece that speaks to you, then create your own design around that one attribute.

I hope you enjoy these jewelry pieces, and wear them while you embrace life, but I hope even more that they inspire you on your own quest for creativity. Start making your own jewelry now and see where the journey takes you.

15642240R00081

Printed in Great Britain
by Amazon